The Complete
Retirement Handbook

The Complete Retirement Handbook

For Anyone Who Will Ever Retire

Forest J. Bowman

Revised Edition

THE UNIVERSITY PRESS OF KENTUCKY

First edition copyright © 1983 by Forest J. Bowman
Revised edition copyright © 1989 by
The University Press of Kentucky

Scholarly publisher for the Commonwealth,
serving Bellarmine College, Berea College, Centre
College of Kentucky, Eastern Kentucky University,
The Filson Club, Georgetown College, Kentucky
Historical Society, Kentucky State University,
Morehead State University, Murray State University,
Northern Kentucky University, Transylvania University,
University of Kentucky, University of Louisville,
and Western Kentucky University.

Editorial and Sales Offices: Lexington, Kentucky 40506

Library of Congress Cataloging-in-Publication Data

Bowman, Forest J.
  The complete retirement handbook : for anyone who will ever retire
/ Forest J. Bowman. — Rev. ed.
      p.   cm.
  ISBN 978-0-8131-5138-0
  1. Retirement—Economic aspects—United States. I. Title.
HQ1063.2.U6B68   1989   89-22758
646.7'9—dc20   CIP

To My, Greg, and Matt, who put up with so
much in seeing this project through

Contents

Acknowledgments

I would like to express my special thanks to the following people for their help with this revised edition: to Nan Impink and Lisa Michel, students at the University of Pittsburgh School of Law, who did much of the research necessary for updating the book; to Rick Briggs and Betty Maxwell at the West Virginia University Gerontology Center for their support and encouragement in putting together a second edition; to Dr. Nancy L. Lohmann, assistant vice president for Academic Affairs at West Virginia University, for constantly encouraging me to keep up my interest in gerontology; and to my wife, Myla, for her undying support and encouragement in putting up with yet another book.

Preface

Retirement is one of life's watershed experiences. Traditionally in our society, it is regarded as the act of shedding the workaday burdens of our lives and taking a well-earned rest, the assumption being that the retiree, enfeebled by something called old age, has officially begun the steady decline toward death. Other societies set their elderly afloat on ice floes or bury them alive; we give them a gold watch and a retirement dinner and then expect them to fade quietly into the background.

Recent research supports what careful observers have noted for some time: The stereotypes about the mental and physical deterioration of retired people are just not true. Nothing automatically happens to the human body at age sixty-five (or at another special age) which suddenly causes its owner to be unable to cope with life or to be less capable of enjoying life's pleasures.

We know now that working capacity does not automatically decline with age; that older people are not less intelligent than younger people; and that verbal abilities and stored information patterns do not decline with age. (In fact, some studies suggest that in many people of better-than-average capacity, learning functions tend to improve with age.)

One thing does not improve with age and retirement: finances. Most Americans enter retirement with inadequate funds for self-support. While it is generally agreed that most retirees could manage comfortably on two thirds to three fourths of their preretirement income, most have less than half that amount. Fully two thirds are forced to live below comfortable income levels.

Moreover, most retirees have not made adequate psychological and emotional preparation for the trauma which retirement often entails. Some studies have found, for example, that as few as 10 percent of retirees were properly prepared. Without adequate preparation, the role disruption, relocation, destruction of long-established social ties at work, and loss of job-acquired status can be devastating.

One way to avoid the profoundly negative effects so often brought on by retirement is to *plan and prepare for the retirement role.*

In a sense, planning for retirement is no different from making preparations for a trip. You plan where you want to go, what you want to do, how much it is likely to cost, and when you want to leave. You study books and pamphlets and maps and guides. You set money aside and arrange your finances carefully. Then you make final plans and reservations, and in some instances, you may even make a dry run.

The same sort of careful advance planning and preparation is necessary for successful retirement. And that, in a nutshell, is what this book is all about.

The Complete
Retirement Handbook

1

It's Your Life— You Call the Shots

WHAT IS RETIREMENT PLANNING?

The term "retirement planning" has no precise definition. It is, rather, a very broad description applied to a great many activities which help us make the adjustment from involvement in the workaday world to a life of leisure and ease—"the last of life, for which the first was made," as Robert Browning put it.

Obviously a life of leisure and ease will require adequate income, so financial planning is a large part of retirement planning. Too much leisure and ease, on the other hand, could become unbearably boring, so part-time work, hobbies, volunteer work with a school or charity, and other activities must also be part of retirement planning.

No amount of leisure and ease will be worth very much if one is in poor health, so maintaining physical and emotional health is an integral part of retirement planning. Indeed, just about any activity that helps us shift gears and prepare for a productive, happy life after leaving full-time employment could be said to be part of retirement planning.

Although it may seem gloomy to think about old age while we're still young, it actually takes a long time to lay the groundwork for a truly successful retirement. Many financial planners and pension consultants advise that it's best to start such planning around age thirty-five. Certainly the financial aspects of retirement planning should be well underway by the time one reaches age forty-five, for the simple reason that the accumulation of adequate funds for retirement is essentially a matter of saving small sums of money over a substantial period of time. Even if you have come to the matter of retirement planning relatively late, there are still a great many things that can be accomplished in a brief period of time.

The single most important factor is the recognition that successful retirement *requires* planning. It doesn't just happen. The person who comes to this conclusion early and begins planning while still in early middle age will obviously have some advantages over the one who arrives at this decision much later, say in his early sixties. An important first step is simply recognizing that there are certain things that can be done in advance to ease the transition.

Someone once said that life is just one damn thing after another. That's obviously a very pessimistic way of thinking. It could also be said that life is a continuing cycle of accidents to which we adjust and which have placed us in our present circumstances. But that presupposes that we have no control over our destiny. Obviously some of us are blessed with better luck than others, but even luck itself is thought by many to be a matter of being ready to take advantage of opportunities when they arise.

So *now* is the time to start planning—not tomorrow or next week or next year. And the logical first step is to establish some goals.

ESTABLISHING RETIREMENT GOALS

Establishing goals means answering a series of questions, the answers to which often lead to even more questions.

Do You *Want* to Retire?

To answer this question, sit down with a sheet of paper divided into two columns: (1) Reasons to Retire, and (2) Reasons Not to

Retire. In each column, list the reasons that apply. Be specific. For example, if one of your reasons for retiring is "free time," ask yourself: free time for what? Then list those purposes. When you've worked the lists over for a week or two, reorganize them into categories. You'll probably find that there will be only one or two *major* factors in each column. If you don't want to retire, for example, it will probably be for only one or two reasons (money, lack of outside interests, etc.), despite the actual number of items on the list. Then balance the reasons for retirement against those opposing it. Ask yourself, Are my reasons realistic? Do I *really* want to sail around the world? Am I *really* so vital to my company that I can't leave? Discuss the lists with your spouse and get his or her honest assessment. Then arrive at a tentative decision.

If your decision is not to retire, find out if there is an age at which you *must* retire from your present job (if you want to stay in this job). The Federal Age Discrimination in Employment Act has extended the mandatory retirement age from sixty-five to seventy in most jobs and protects people who are still at work against arbitrary discrimination because of age. This means you cannot be pressured to retire—threatened, forced to take a lesser job, given fewer privileges, or paid less than or treated differently from younger workers. If you decide to retire from your present job but still want to work, this law protects you from being discriminated against by a prospective employer solely on the basis of age, unless being of a specific age is a bona fide qualification for the job. The American Bar Association booklet *Your Rights Over Age 50,* which is available for $2 from the Circulation Department, American Bar Association, 1155 East 60 Street, Chicago, IL 60637, gives the details of this law and would be a good investment.

When you are thinking about alternative "postretirement" jobs, don't overlook self-employment, perhaps through expansion of a hobby into a serious part-time job. Or consider the possibility of making special retirement use of job-related expertise which you can convert into a source of retirement employment.

Once you have decided whether to retire, the remaining questions are the same, regardless of your decision. For example, if you choose not to retire but to develop your photography hobby into a part-time business, you still have to decide where to live, how much money you'll need, and the like. And even if you decide to stay right in your present job without moving or changing your income level, you'll still need to begin planning for the time when you must leave that job.

As you decide whether you really want to retire or whether you want to continue with some sort of work, you must never lose sight of your uniqueness. It is trite but nonetheless true that in all the world, there has never been anyone like you before and there will be no one like you when you are gone. So you need to plan for a retirement that will satisfy you and you alone. (This is not to say you should ignore your spouse, but part of the relationship with your spouse should be that you share likes and dislikes.)

One guide to remember in retirement planning is the realization that we seldom change our likes and dislikes. You'll probably like and dislike the same things in retirement that you do now. The fact is, you are what you are now, you are what you were, and you are what you will be. Just as the past is the key to your present, so the past and the present are keys to your future. Successful decisions regarding retirement depend upon understanding your past likes and dislikes.

When to Retire

According to the United States Office of Vital Statistics, men sixty-five years of age can expect to live another 14.6 years, and women 18.6 years. At age fifty-five, men have a life expectancy of 21.5 years, and women 26.6 years. At age fifty, men have an average life expectancy of 25.6 years, and women 30.9 years. So you are going to be planning for a large chunk of your life.

Depending on the particulars of individual retirement plans, most Americans may retire at age fifty-five by taking reduced benefits or may remain employed up to age seventy and then retire with maximum benefits. The trade-off is, of course, that if you retire at age fifty-five you will take lower monthly benefits for the rest of your life, but you will have a longer period to enjoy the benefits you do receive. If you work longer, on the other hand, you will receive benefits for a shorter period of time, but the monthly payments will be larger.

One of the factors in determining when to retire will be, of course, your present job satisfaction. Another will be how ready you are financially to retire at an age earlier than the traditional sixty-five.

The true retirement financial picture, as we shall see later, also involves taking into account your spouse's potential retirement income and trying to determine the optimum time for either or both of you to retire so that both may enjoy the maximum benefits for the longest period of time.

It may be, for example, that you will want to work until age sixty-five and permit your wife,[1] who is three years younger, to retire at age sixty-two. Thus while she will take a slightly lower benefit, she can synchronize her retirement with yours and the two of you together can have an adequate retirement income. If, on the other hand, there is a substantial difference in age between you and your wife, it may be advisable for your wife to work for some time after you have retired. This, of course, will have some impact on the question to *where* to retire, because unless your wife can obtain ready employment without a loss of pension privileges in a new retirement home, it will be necessary to remain in the old home until she retires.

When to retire is perhaps the most important question for one who has decided to retire. Nevertheless, the answer to this question is quite often dictated by other factors, such as health and income. As a general rule, one should retire early (i.e., before mandatory retirement or at least before age 65) only if the following conditions are present:

1. You have no major financial responsibilities which you cannot meet without your regular income.
2. You are qualified to receive Social Security payments at age 62 or age 65.
3. You are covered by a company, union, or private medical plan that will protect you until you are qualified for Medicare benefits at age 65.
4. You will be able, by the terms of your retirement, to work elsewhere should you decide later that you want to do so.

---

1. In this book, we will be talking about the husband and wife from the husband's viewpoint as the older marriage partner. We will also be looking at tax and estate planning from the same position and assuming that the husband dies first. This viewpoint is not taken from a chauvinistic attitude but rather from a reflection that men more commonly than women marry a younger partner, and statistically the husband dies first. But it is important to understand that the rules are equally applicable if the wife should be older and retire or die first.

5. You have carefully weighed all the advantages and disadvantages—financial, physical, medical, and psychological—and are certain that early retirement is the thing for you.

What to Do in Retirement

Another major question is: what do you plan to do with your time in retirement? One of the joys of retirement is supposedly the right to choose to do whatever you wish. But most of us need some sort of structure, however loosely developed, around which to pattern the use of our time. Boredom is a major factor in the aging process of retired persons. "Leisure" is not the same thing as "idleness," and some of the most ageless retirees are those who appear to be the busiest. In reality, they are merely doing what they enjoy immensely and what their time and income allow them to do without restriction.

So as you begin to plan for retirement, you need to consider carefully just what you might want to do with your time. This decision, like most other decisions regarding retirement, need not be cast in concrete. You can decide, for example, that you want to spend your retirement hunting and fishing, then later turn to something else as you weary of those activities or become interested in other pastimes. There is absolutely nothing wrong with trying out various avocations as long as you understand that the major concern is being able to provide yourself with meaningful activity after retirement. And the important thing is to begin *now* to think of ways to keep yourself positively occupied.

How you live in retirement will determine your happiness. You can pick the right time and the right place, you can have adequate funds, you can be healthy and alert, and you can have a spouse tuned in to your retirement needs and willing to cooperate all the way. But unless you have a meaningful plan for the use of your leisure time, your retirement will not be successful.

Note that you are not trying to determine how to keep yourself occupied *all the time* during retirement, but rather to give yourself something meaningful to do on those occasions when "doing nothing" begins to weigh heavily on you. Nothing is sadder than seeing someone retire after a lifetime of hard, productive work and then watching that person spend all his or her time waiting for the grass to grow so it can be cut again to take up at least a few hours of seemingly endless time. It is this sort of boredom that leads to psychosomatic illness, overdrinking, and severe depression.

PRACTICING FOR RETIREMENT

The preretirement period is an ideal time to begin trying out some possible retirement activities. If you think you might like to travel and perhaps do some hunting and fishing along the way, why not rent a camper and take an extended vacation some summer to try these activities? If you think you might like to take up golf, do it now. Don't wait until retirement. Also, you can double up in your research. For example, the questions of what you will do in retirement and where you want to retire can be worked out together. If you plan, for example, to move to Florida and spend some time fishing there, now is the ideal time to vacation in Florida and try out the waters.

Partial or gradual retirement may provide some answers to the questions about where to retire and what to do with your time. It may also offer an opportunity to adjust gradually to the abrupt change from work to full-time leisure. Gradual retirement, if it can be worked out with your employer, permits you to reduce work time and increase vacation time, with a corresponding reduction in pay. This allows you to begin role playing for retirement and also gives your employer the use of your expertise and permits the company to move other employees into your position in a training capacity. There can then be less stress and trauma all around. If gradual retirement is done properly, you can find yourself in the midst of a successful retirement almost without realizing it.

You begin, then, by gathering all the information available on your retirement options and weighing various possibilities against your present inclinations. Talk to others with whom you work about their plans, about people they may know who live in the places where you're thinking about moving and who do the things you plan to do after retirement. Visit your public library and inquire about the localities you are interested in and the avocations you may want to pursue. Talk to your lawyer and accountant and your company's pension advisers about various ages of retirement and what effect they will have on your pension and

Social Security income and the like. Then, once you have decided with some degree of finality (remembering always that one of the pleasures of doing this sort of planning is that you have the right to change your mind), begin working directly to achieve your goal.

Let's assume you decide that the answer to your first question is yes—you do want to retire. Second, you decide that you want to retire along the coast of South Carolina at age sixty-five to fish and play golf. What next?

Well, you are merely at the second level of questions which must be answered. You have to know now how much money you will need to make up the difference between your retirement income (about which more later) and what you will need to live on in the area of South Carolina you have chosen. You need to know about the availability of housing you want and can afford in that area. Here, again, you need some expert advice. Visit those areas of South Carolina and talk with realtors, bankers, and representatives of local chambers of commerce. Learn what is available. See what you can afford. See what appeals to you and what turns you off. As you do all this, you may decide you do not want to live in South Carolina after all. Or you may realize that you would soon tire of fishing and golfing and may change your plans entirely. Fine. Now is the time to do this. It's much easier than trying to undo established plans after you retire.

If you do change your mind, go back to square one; start asking the same questions again and work your way forward. As you determine with some degree of finality *what* you want to do, *where* you want to do it, and *when* you want to do it, you must then concentrate on the answers. Next determine what financial resources you have available and what you will need, and decide whether there is an unreasonable gap between them.

YOUR RETIREMENT ADVISERS

Along the way, perhaps the most valuable asset you can acquire is a group of professional advisers who will help you answer these questions. If you look at the questions, you will see that they are of two sorts. First, there are the personal ones which have to do with the sort of climate you like and your hobbies and interests; and second, there are the financial questions. You need, then, a general retirement adviser or two as well as someone to give advice on financial matters. Selecting financial advisers is perhaps the easiest task you face, because you probably have several already. Your insurance broker, your banker, your mutual funds salesperson, your stockbroker, your company's pension adviser—all these people can help prepare you financially for retirement.

Another very important adviser is your lawyer. The right lawyer can provide you with extensive information on various aspects of the law as it affects the retiree.

Finding a lawyer is much like finding a doctor. Your best bet is always to ask others for recommendations based on their own personal experience. If this doesn't work—because you're new in the community or no one you know has used a lawyer for the purpose you have in mind—check the *Martindale Hubbell Directory of Lawyers*, which is in most public libraries. This four-volume work contains a great deal of information on lawyers, including age, education, whether they are associated with other lawyers, and a rating by their peers as to legal ability and general reliability. The listings are geographical. There are also directories of specialists—probate counsel, collection lawyers, patent attorneys, negligence lawyers, bank counsel, and the like. These directories can usually be found in the law library at your local courthouse.

As to advisers for other types of questions—the personal questions—you are left more to your own devices. Part of the fun of planning for retirement is learning how to ferret out answers to personal questions in ingenious ways. One of the pleasant side effects of all this planning is that often these personal advisers become extremely close friends as your reliance on them grows and develops.

ONE FINAL WORD

But shouldn't you have the right to depend on the government and your employer to provide you with proper retirement planning and, indeed, to provide you with a satisfactory retirement? Unless you are employed in a position not covered by Social Security, you will be paying into the Social Security Fund. So shouldn't the government take care of your retirement financial needs through Social Security? Shouldn't you be able to depend upon Congress to see that the Social Security Fund remains fiscally strong throughout your retirement? And shouldn't you be able to rely on Congress to see that your employer maintains the proper retirement fund for you?

The answer to all these questions is, of course, yes. But they are really not the questions you should be asking. The real question is not whether you *should* be able to depend on the government or your employer but whether you *can*. And only a blind, staggering fool would depend on anyone but himself for the ultimate protection in retirement. Only someone who has not read a newspaper and watched the government in action for the past quarter century or who does not understand that business has higher priorities than providing retirement planning for its aging employees would depend on government or business for his future.

Only *you* can provide adequate retirement planning for yourself. This is not to say that the government and your employer are evil or unfeeling or unconcerned about your future. It is simply a reflection of the fact that if you are going to have a successful retirement, you must plan that retirement and, in large part, you must fund that retirement.

The liberal agenda has failed us. It has provided us with vast, expensive social welfare programs which have resulted in persistent inflation. The conservative agenda has failed us. It has provided us with high unemployment and economic recession. All this has happened not because our representatives in Washington or in our state capitals are unfeeling and unconcerned but because they are basically concerned with one issue: reelection. (Most of them believe, quite honestly, that their own reelection is essential to the welfare of the state or country.) Anyone who relies on this kind of leadership to provide for his future is a fool.

Social Security, in my judgment, as I will explain later, will be around for the long run in some form. Pension protection is now a matter of national law and will stay with us. But no one except you can assure that government- and business-sponsored programs are going to be very meaningful in the long run.

Only you can determine when you want to retire, where you want to retire, how much money you will need for retirement, and what you will do in retirement. Only you can assure through a careful, systematic savings program that you will have the necessary funds.

If, upon your retirement, the government or your company provides you with additional funds—hallelujah! You can tell your wife, "Look, dear, here's a nice check from the government." Fine. But anything you get from the government or your own pension plan must be considered as only part of your overall planning for retirement—even the financial planning.

If all this sounds pessimistic, it is not meant to be. The truth is that none of us has any right to depend on anyone else for anything. We have the obligation to provide for ourselves while we are working and after retirement. And with careful planning, we can do just that.

In all your goal setting and planning for retirement, the major factor to recall always is that it is your life you are planning, and you are the one who should call the shots. Part of the joy of retirement is that you no longer have to listen to bosses and foremen who tell you what to do and when to do it. Now you are free to follow the dictates of your own conscience and your own desires. Now you make your decisions based on your best understanding of all the facts you have rounded up from your advisers and other sources.

The world is your oyster. Make the best of it.

2

Life Begins at Retirement

THE AGING PROCESS

What Happens As the Body Grows Older

Around the age of thirty, all of us begin to go through the process known as aging as we start to lose some of the natural resiliency of youth. The process is a perfectly natural one, although the pace at which it occurs varies from person to person.

Many signs of aging are quite obvious. Near age thirty-five on the average, hair begins to go gray as some hairs lose their natural pigmentation. The process is gradual until finally there are more white hairs than hairs of the original color and we are no longer said to be gray but white-haired. About the same time, baldness develops in many men, for which as yet there is no known cure.

Wrinkles begin to appear in middle age as the skin loses its elasticity. Some of the fat underlying the skin is lost, and so the outer skin has less support below the surface. Except for cosmetic surgery, there is no known cure for the wrinkling process, although avoidance of excessive exposure to sun, excessive exposure to soap and water, and frowning and exaggerated facial expressions can prevent acceleration of the wrinkling process.

Hearing and vision begin to decline at about age forty. Presbyopia, a condition in which the lens of the eye loses the ability to accommodate for near and distant vision, causes many persons to adopt reading glasses or bifocals. Later—usually not until advanced old age—vision-impairing opaque spots known as cataracts appear on the lens and interfere with vision. They are, however, correctable by surgery; today cataract surgery is one of the more common sorts of surgery for the elderly.

Hearing does not deteriorate much with age with regard to everyday sounds, but presbycusis, an inability to distinguish high-frequency sounds (10,000 cycles per second or higher), occurs more often as we age. There is some reason to believe this condition may be environmentally related—that is, it may be due to lifetime exposure to high noise levels. Some of the elderly also are affected by otosclerosis, a condition that results in the hardening of a middle-ear bone, leaving it unable to transmit sounds effectively. This condition, too, is correctable by surgery.

Taste and smell tend to diminish somewhat with age, though not markedly so. Perhaps because the decline is so gradual, most elderly people are unaware of their loss of sensitivity. There is also some reason to believe that age alone is not responsible for this deterioration. In many instances, a lifetime of smoking or a recent disease may cause the condition. Some people may suffer from a disturbance in thyroid-gland function or a deficiency in body levels of zinc, both of which are correctable with medication.

Muscle strength begins to diminish after the mid-twenties. Athletes commonly are at their peak before thirty and are considered old by forty. Between the ages of twenty and eighty, the volume of air that can be taken in and expelled by the lungs drops by 40 percent and the amount of oxygen passing into the blood is decreased by about 50 percent. The lungs lose some of their elasticity, and their efficiency decreases. The bony cage covering the lungs stiffens, and the muscles used to move the chest weaken so that less air is moved in and out of the lungs.

However, aging again may not be the real culprit. Regular exercise can increase the efficiency of the lungs and improve the operation of the muscles that move the chest, all of which helps get air in and out of the lungs. Obesity and cigarette smoking also impair lung function. (Interestingly, when smoking is stopped, lung function returns to near normal for age level within a year and a half to two years.) Studies indicate that between the ages of twenty and ninety, the amount of blood pumped to the heart declines by 50 percent, although the number of beats per minute remains virtually the same in people at rest. Again, however, if the older heart is free of disease, exercise can have a significant effect in improving the capacity of the heart to pump blood.

The kidneys eventually lose up to 50 percent of their operating capacity. The kidneys filter waste from the body in the form of urine, and they require greater volumes of water to do this as we age. However, in the healthy kidney, there is considerable reserve tissue, and so even a loss of up to 50 percent of kidney capacity should not interfere with adequate function.

The digestive system slows down. Adrenaline production also slows down, resulting, perhaps, in a lowered ability of the aged to respond to stress. The body loses some of its efficiency in reducing excess blood sugar. The production of sex hormones ebbs. Reduced intestinal contractions may contribute to constipation.

We age, at least in part, because our immune system wears out. This system is at its peak during puberty and declines to one tenth of that efficiency in old age. Many of the diseases common to old age—cancer, arthritis, and vascular disease, to name only three—are thought to be in some way the result of a declining immune system.

All in all, then, the body simply begins to wear out beginning sometime after age thirty. There may be, of course, a physiological reason for this. Humankind is "biologically unnecessary" after about the age of thirty if we assume that a man and woman can reproduce themselves at about age fifteen and that they should remain alive to protect their offspring until the offspring are about age fifteen.

However, while bodily functions may decrease and we may undergo profound alterations internally and externally, few people die literally of old age—wearing out. Life span has increased dramatically throughout the world since 1900. Biologically speaking, there is no reason why human beings cannot have an average life span at some time of 110 to 120 years. So aging is a condition that we all face, but it is not necessarily a terminal condition. There are studies that suggest that the ability to age gracefully—to accept the changes and to adapt mentally to the changing body—is an important factor in how happy we will be in later life.

YOUR FAMILY MEDICAL HISTORY

There is considerable new evidence, widely accepted within the scientific community, that a tendency toward some diseases or physical conditions may run in families. For example, the occurrence of heart disease, stroke, cancer, hypertension, and even alcoholism has been found to have some sort of genetic factor. This suggests that all of us—and especially those who are nearing the age when normal body immunities may be somewhat reduced—should have a clear understanding of our family medical history. Moreover, the importance of starting early has been emphasized. A few years ago, the American Heart Association recommended that children in families with a high risk of heart and blood-vessel disease be examined by a doctor and placed on a corrective diet if they are found to have excessive blood fat levels.

These recent findings should not be surprising, since other disorders and diseases have long been known to be genetically related (for example, hemophilia, a genetic disorder that is passed on from mother to daughter—though its effects are seen in male children of carriers, not usually in female children).

We all should keep complete records of our health and medical history, know as much as possible about the health and medical condition of our ancestors, and pass this information on to our children and grandchildren for their benefit. Knowing that we have a tendency toward a heart condition, for example, can permit us to take steps that are widely recognized as reducing the risk of heart disease, such as losing weight, exercising, and not smoking.

RULES FOR HEALTHY LIVING

The Human Population Laboratory of the California Department of Health Services, which has been studying the residents of Alameda County since 1965, has recommended Seven Rules of Clean Living for health and longevity:

1. Get the right amount of sleep. (The amount varies from person to person but is generally 8 hours for men, 7 for women.)
2. Eat a good breakfast each day.
3. Eat three meals a day at regular times and avoid snacks.
4. Exercise regularly (preferably in some kind of sport).

29

5. Control weight.
6. Drink moderately (no more than one or two drinks a day).
7. Don't smoke cigarettes.[1]

To these rules we might also add: Be married. Statistics indicate that married people are by and large biologically a lot younger than unmarried people of the same age. (By "marriage" we mean a happy marriage, for an unhappy marriage could have a negative effect on physical and mental health.)

The age at which your ancestors died may give some hint to your general condition and longevity. However, as a practical matter, being a member of a family in which longevity is typical probably suggests at best a lessened likelihood that genetic deficiencies have been passed along.

Exercise, one of the Seven Rules of Clean Living, clearly has an effect in reversing many of the physiological conditions among older people. Suitable exercise, for example, can increase blood-circulation efficiency, restore muscle tone, increase lung capacity, and enable the heart to pump more blood regularly.

Diet plays a major role in health at any age. However, the effect of diet is exaggerated as we grow older. The metabolic rate—that is, the rate at which the body burns calories—declines regularly as we age. Moreover, food-calorie needs drop even more because of decreased physical activity. The combination of decreased activity and decline in metabolic rate means that unless we reduce our food intake and maintain an exercise program as we grow older, obesity is just around the corner.

FINDING THE RIGHT DOCTOR

All the previous suggestions involve self-diagnosis and self-treatment. It is equally important as you age that you find the right kind of medical care. Choosing a doctor is one of the most important health decisions you'll ever make. So be careful.

1. Ask a friend, relative, or neighbor to recommend a doctor. If you have just moved into a new area and don't know anyone, call the county or state medical society and ask for a list of recommended

1. Courtesy of the Human Population Laboratory, California Department of Health Services. These items were developed under research grant support from the National Center for Health Services Research, US Department of Health and Human Services.

doctors. Before you move, ask your present physician to recommend a physician in the new community or to give you some advice on locating one.

2. Once you have the name of a physician, make an appointment with that doctor. Discuss with him your medical needs—what you are looking for in a doctor—and see if he can meet those needs. Find out if he makes house calls and at what hospital he practices. What about patient care on weekends and holidays and after office hours? What are his fees?

3. Select a doctor who can personally take care of most of your medical problems. Do not limit yourself to a specialist but find a doctor who delivers primary medical care. In recent years, the specialty known as family practice has been growing by leaps and bounds. This specialty includes general practitioners (that is, doctors of medicine) who spend three years following medical school learning to provide basic medical care to all members of the family—old and young, male and female. For general medical needs, a family-practice specialist is often a good choice.

4. Make certain that your doctor is properly qualified. It might be to your advantage to select someone who is "board-certified," a doctor who has taken additional training and has passed an examination given by that specialty's board of examiners. But the primary thing is to make certain that your doctor is a certified physician who is properly licensed and recognized by the state medical authorities as being qualified to treat patients.

5. Choose someone you like. This is an emotional matter, but you should feel at ease discussing any medical problems you may have with your doctor. If you don't feel comfortable with him, even though you can't put your finger on just why, seek another physician.

6. Once you have located a doctor, cooperate fully with him. He can help you only if he knows the full facts of your medical past and any problems you may have. Concealing problems from your doctor because you are embarrassed can only impede his efforts to help you. The truth is that doctors, like lawyers and ministers, are very hard to embarrass, having seen and heard it all. So if you've been fortunate enough to find a doctor with whom you are pleased, do everything you can to help him do the best for you.

COST OF MEDICAL CARE

Medicare pays less than 40 percent of the health-care costs of the elderly, and inflation is likely to erode these benefits further.

You will need, then, supplemental medical insurance after retirement. Preventive care is highly important, so you need to know if you can continue with protection under your present employer's group medical insurance plan or if it will be necessary to buy private medical coverage.

COPING WITH ILL HEALTH

We humans cope with ill health in fashions as varied as our own personalities. For some, ill health is the end of the road, and the slightest physical disorder can bring them to a screeching halt. For others, it's just another one of those minor things that get in the way. It is becoming clearer than ever that certain conditions can be cured and others must be endured, but life need not stop because of physical disorders.

If you suffer from irreversible disorders which cause conditions as varied as palsy, decreased mobility, or loss of sight or hearing, then you have but two choices—to go on living as normal and productive a life as possible or to cave in and let the condition overwhelm you. Abraham Lincoln once said, "Most people are just about as happy as they make up their minds to be." That's a pretty good rule for dealing with ill health.

So, also, when a spouse becomes seriously ill or dies, life must go on. For the surviving partner or the healthy partner to become a martyr to a spouse's illness or death is to violate everything that the relationship with the spouse should have stood for.

In caring for an ill spouse, it is important to try to maintain some semblance of an orderly life of one's own, not turning your back on the ill partner but understanding that a certain amount of normal living is absolutely essential for physical and mental health. This is not to say that a husband whose wife is dying should date other women and paint the town red. But the husband should not simply sit by the wife's bedside, hold her hand, and cry. To enable the wife to endure a debilitating illness, it is essential that the husband maintain all the physical and mental strength he possibly can. Maintaining a reasonable degree of normal activity is absolutely essential.

Also, after the death of a spouse, it is important to resume some semblance of normalcy. This does not mean rushing out to remarry before one has had the time to review the situation carefully. Neither does it mean living alone surrounded by memories of a loved one who has passed on. Time does not erase wounds, but it heals them, and the healing process can be speeded up and strengthened by maintaining a normal life and thinking of the future.

OLD AND SENILE?

The myth that human intellectual capacity peaks in the early twenties and then diminishes is apparently just that—a myth. Recent studies suggest that aging in and of itself appears to have no detrimental effect on learning ability and IQ. General intelligence can be maintained well into old age, and, indeed, there are some indications that it increases as the person continues to be active.

However, if the overall health of the individual declines, mental capacity appears to decline, too. As with health generally, mental condition appears to be a factor that is largely determined by how an old person views life in general and determines to face it. If you view life as one continuing series of problems and you expect the very worst to come your way, then your general physical and mental health will probably decline. If, on the other hand, you view retirement as an opportunity to try the things you have always wanted to do but never had the time to, and you are willing to ignore the minor physical problems that inevitably accompany aging, there is no reason to experience any decline in mental capacity, given reasonably good health.

My father died at the age of eighty-one. For years he suffered from arteriosclerosis, congestive heart failure, black lung, cancer of the prostate, and bleeding ulcers. He did what his physician told him to do and did not dwell on the fact that he had serious health problems. Until he developed a terminal illness and died over a period of three months, he was as mentally alert as he had ever been in his life. My mother is eighty. Forty-five years ago, she was some sixty pounds overweight. Determined that she was not going to spend her life as a fat woman, she lost all her excess weight gradually and carefully over a period of two to three years. She has maintained excellent physical condition, despite a few setbacks along the way such as shingles, bursitis, and a gallbladder operation. Today she enrolls in every adult-education class

33

the local high school offers. She has taken up upholstering, oil painting, and early-American theorem painting (painting with stencils on velvet) and is the oldest and fittest person in her exercise class. She walks at least a mile a day or rides an exercise bike when the weather is bad.

My mother has many friends and visits extensively. While she hasn't a great deal of money, she and my father planned carefully for their retirement, and my mother has adequate funds to live on. Her life is busier and more involved than ever before. I am convinced that this plays an important role in her good health.

I had a great-great-aunt who died in her hundred-and-first year. When I first met her, I was disappointed that she did not tell me more tales of her youth when she was a playmate of my grandmother, who died when I was very young. But as I watched this ninety-nine-year-old woman run up the stairs to locate some photographs of her grandchildren for me, I realized that she—like my parents—was alive and well at an advanced age because she chose not to live in the past but to live for tomorrow. Physical health, intellectual capacity, you name it; it is largely a factor of mind over matter.

CHANGING FOCUS: RETIREMENT INVOLVEMENT

There is a condition known as the retirement syndrome, a conglomeration of real or imagined ailments that afflict some but not all retirees. Dr. Robert M. Butler, in his book *Why Survive? Being Old in America*, says that "men and women who are otherwise perfectly healthy sometimes develop headaches, gastrointestinal symptoms, oversleeping, irritability, nervousness, and lethargy." Other folks become happier and healthier after retirement. The difference appears to lie in how well you adjust to the business of retirement.

Ideally, retirement ought to involve giving up *part* of life—that is, the profession or occupation that we pursue to earn our daily bread—and replacing it with interests for which we had only a little time while we were working. The ideal, unfortunately, is easier written about than achieved.

Perhaps the most difficult obstacle to a successful retirement is letting go of what we have in our workaday life. For some, it's giving up the power they have, through the job they hold, over other people whose jobs they direct or over others in the community with whom they come in contact. For almost all retirees, there is some loss of income (though that need not be as difficult as when there has been no careful financial planning). This loss of money in itself leads to a loss of status.

Ask the typical American male who he is and he will respond not by giving his name or the name of his family but by telling you what he does for a living. This perhaps more than anything else suggests how serious is this problem of preparing for retirement. You must be prepared to accept a different status upon retirement. But it need not be a lesser or an inferior status to that which you held when you worked. You have merely shifted focus, and now instead of spending your time doing someone else's bidding at a job or profession in which your major concern was earning enough to provide for your family's keep, you can do what you want. (If this is a reduction in status, most of us would gladly accept the reduction in return for the advantages.)

Being Needed

For most of us, the real feeling of loss in status comes not so much from the loss of any particular status or position we held in our workaday lives as from a sudden feeling that we are no longer needed.

Retirement need not mean we are unnecessary to others. Indeed, one of the great advantages of retirement is having the time to help people in ways that we find satisfying to ourselves. Retirement, then, is the time for community endeavors. Get involved in the local school-board election or the local grass-roots political organization of a presidential candidate. Offer yourself as an instructor for high-school or community-college courses that relate to your lifetime work.

Making yourself available to help others may also mean extra money in your pocket. For example, assume that you were an accountant. Now when income-tax time approaches, you have all the time in the world to prepare simple tax returns. You might offer yourself as an employee to H & R Block or some other similar national tax preparer. Or you might simply hang out a little sign and offer yourself as a tax preparer, after carefully checking the local laws on such a business.

Or if your work involves machinist skills, offer to teach a few hours a week at the local vocational school. Your kind of experience is precisely what students of those schools will value more than any number of academic degrees. You'll find a new sense of esteem, and you'll probably be paid more than you expect.

What if you have worked in a field that is highly esoteric and not adaptable to retirement life? For instance, assume you were an infantry officer in the United States Army all your working life. Do you have to sit behind the desk of a motel as a night clerk? Of course not. An infantry officer's leadership skills are extremely valuable and highly sought after by people organizing all sorts of activities. Or suppose you worked as a clerk in a government office, filing records and retrieving them on demand. You could hire yourself out as a genealogist whose job is essentially researching government records to find traces of families.

The point of all this is that your past life is not over—your present life is just an opportunity to improve on it. What you enjoyed most from your work can be built into a hobby or vocation. What you didn't enjoy and are glad to have past can be left behind.

The government even helps a bit. There are significant tax breaks for volunteers who itemize their deductions on individual income tax returns. For example, if your volunteer work requires you to wear a uniform, you can claim the purchase price and the cleaning bills as deductions. Although you may not claim a charitable-contribution deduction for the value of the unpaid work you perform for a charity, you can deduct out-of-pocket expenses such as the cost of telephone calls, stamps and stationery and the materials you use to make anything used by the charity, such as the cost of baking for a cookie sale. You may deduct travel expenses whether you go by bus, train, taxi, or car. If your volunteer work requires being away from home overnight, you may deduct a reasonable amount for meals and lodging. (For specific information on deductions for volunteer work, IRS publication No. 526, *Income Tax Deductions for Contributions*, is invaluable.)

So change your focus in retirement. Do what you want to do— but do something! Taking life easy doesn't mean just sitting around and soaking up the sun. It means doing something meaningful with what is left of your life. And if you do it right, there is apt to be a great deal left of your life after retirement.

YOU AND YOUR SPOUSE

Remember the time when you once dreamed romantically of spending all your time together—of never being separated? Then you got married. You had to go off to work and your spouse had to go off to work or had the demanding job of maintaining a home and caring for young children.

Now it's retirement time, and you can finally realize that romantic dream. *Don't do it!* This romantic dream carries certain seeds of disaster.

The fact is that all of us need time alone. Husband and wife may be close, but they need separation occasionally. No matter how much a man and woman grow together, they also retain their basic differences. The lives of men and women are shaped differently, so that almost inevitably each married partner has interests and skills the other does not have. This is not bad but rather is the strength of the marriage, and each partner needs the time to pursue these interests and skills separately.

Someone once wrote that if two people agree on everything, one of them is unnecessary. This is, of course, especially true of a married couple. No marriage, even one strongly bound by love and respect, can survive the monotony of total togetherness. So give your partner some room and time to be alone.

Consideration

Also, remember that in a marriage that has lasted many years, there can be a tendency to overlook the needs and concerns of the other partner. As we grow older and suffer some of the physical ailments that usually come with age, we tend to suffer loudly at home, but out of the house, we are hail-fellow-well-met. The truth is, however, that the delightful, charming person our friends see and admire can become a boring, overbearing, dependent pain in the neck at home. So give your spouse the same sort of consideration you give to friends or even total strangers.

Treat your spouse with respect—give him or her room to live an independent life, and try to make that life easier. For example, a common problem or complaint of retirement is that the man retires from his job but the wife still has all the burdens of running a home and so is never able to retire. Retirement, then, is the time for the husband to take on some of the burdens of helping around the house.

And don't let your appearance go to pot just because you're retired and are not out in the world all the time. Our own appearance reflects how we feel about ourselves. People feel much better about themselves if they dress to reflect the best in them.

So don't shuffle around the house in night clothing until the afternoon. Men should get up, shave, and dress. Women should take their hair out of curlers, throw off the bathrobe, and get dressed for the day. Don't make do with casual clothing that you purchased at a yard sale fifteen years ago. With time now to take advantage of sales at all times of the year, watch for a few items of stylish clothing and keep your wardrobe going in a way that satisfactorily reflects a proper image of yourself.

There is nothing wrong with growing old, and one should not attempt to dress beneath his or her age. Nothing quite reveals the fact that we are growing older so much as attempting to dress younger than we should. Growing old these days doesn't mean donning ill-fitting, out-of-date, shabby clothing. You owe it to yourself and to your spouse to maintain your appearance.

LIVE FOR TODAY

Finally, if you want to have any friends and avoid driving your spouse around the bend, don't live in the past. Most people don't care about our past, and the truth is most of us have pasts that aren't terribly interesting to anyone but ourselves. If someone wants to know about yesterday—about Harry Truman's upset victory in 1948 or what it was like during the Great Depression—fine. Otherwise, live for tomorrow. It's one way to keep yourself young.

3

Sun Belt, Here I Come! Moving After Retirement

Next to when to retire, where to live during retirement is perhaps the most important question facing a prospective retiree. In order to make a wise decision, a careful evaluation of all the possibilities is necessary.

If you are thinking about moving to a new area, be sure to base your selection on your own knowledge of the locality and its advantages for you and not on what someone else has tried to sell you.

You might begin your investigation by looking at *Places Rated Almanac*, by Richard Boyer and David Savageau (Rand McNally, 1981). This book rates 277 metropolitan areas in such categories as climate, economic strength, education, housing, recreation, transportation, crime, and health care. It can help you start to narrow your choice somewhat and to compare your present community with other ones. The book has received widespread attention from the media, and your local library should have a copy.

Also, *Woodall's Sunbelt Retirement Directory*, put out annually by Woodall Publishing Company (500 Hyacinth Place, Highland Park, IL 60035), gives information on general demographics, medical facilities, business opportunities, and the like across the country.

Whether to move or to stay in your preretirement home is, of course, a personal decision. And that decision must be based to some extent on the retirement opportunities that are found in your community; the presence and availability of neighbors, friends, and family on whom you can lean for support; and your own deep-seated feelings about the community, its climate, and its attractiveness as a residence. But if you think you might like to move to a new community in another area of the country, there is a whole laundry list of questions which must be answered to your satisfaction and a number of approaches to acquiring those answers.

1. You need to know about the *climate*. Is it just wonderful in the winter (when the climate back home is lousy) but unbearable in the summer during the off-season?
2. What sort of *convenience* does the area offer in the way of shopping, community activities, churches, medical care, and accessibility to other parts of the country via railroad, bus, or airline?
3. What are the *medical facilities* like? Are they up to date as well as easy to reach from all areas of the community?
4. What is the *public transportation* like? Are the buses clean, the schedules reasonable, and the prices right? You may drive now, but later on, being near a bus line may be a very significant factor for a happy retirement.
5. What are the *personal property* and *real property taxes* like? Are there any tax breaks for the elderly?
6. Are there *elderly communities* within the larger community? What facilities do they offer? Are the people happy there?
7. What *recreational facilities* are available in the community at large? Are they adequate for the community or strained by overuse?
8. What are the *libraries* like? Are there any schools that offer *adult education courses*?
9. Are there any significant factors about the *climate* or the *terrain* or the *vegetation*—anything—that would affect any ailments you or your spouse may have?
10. What do the *cost-of-living statistics* say about this area? How up to date are they?
11. What do the state's *inheritance laws* provide? What is necessary for a valid will in this state?

Obviously, some of these questions will be easier to answer than others. First you need to visit the locality, but don't go just during the high season when the climate is at its best. Visit during off-season. Find out whether you can tolerate the worst of the heat and humidity that the area can offer. If you are interested in New England, go there in the deep snows of winter and find out if you can take the isolation and the cold.

When you visit, talk with people. Don't just go to the tourist attractions but check out the small shops, the libraries, the places where people should be if things are happening in this community. Ask questions. If you move there, you will spend precious little time at the historical monuments but much of your time in these other places. They can tell you a great deal about the community.

Subscribe to the local newspaper to check out community activities, prices, and signs of the presence or absence of violent crime in the community. Try to sense what sort of government the community has.

Write to the chamber of commerce and explain that you are interested in moving to this area and would like some information about it. Be prepared to receive some highly flowery and complimentary information—but it's a good starting point.

Write to the state capital's office on aging (or whatever it may be called in that state) and ask about tax breaks for the elderly, tax laws relating to real and personal property, and inheritance laws.

On your visit to the community, ride the buses, go to the barber or beauty shop, and check out the stores that you would be using as a resident.

Consult a realtor. Realtors know the local neighborhoods, and if you sound like a good prospect, they'll be a wealth of information. Before you visit the community, you can assess the housing market through a realtor in your current area who participates in national multilisting. Check your phone book for this information. Two such organizations are Nationwide Relocation Service and Inter-City Relocation Service. These services will give you some basic information on the community and will put you in touch with a realtor in the community you're interested in.

Check out the grocery stores and see if food prices are compatible with those at home and what if any changes in eating style might be necessitated by the merchandise available and the prices. Find out if the community has any variety of shops or if it has one standardized mall after another.

In short, immerse yourself in the community and get some sense of what it might be like to live there. If, after all this research, you want to live there, try it first. Rent, do not sell, your present home; and when you move to that community, rent, do not buy. Give yourself part of the tourist season and part of the off-season to find out what you really like and dislike about the community, and every week, write down these feelings and the reasons for them. Be specific. Keep adding to the lists week after week. As you review the lists each week, try to determine if there are any patterns to your likes and dislikes. For example, if you discover that your likes are all gushing reviews of local tourist attractions, beware. When you've done it all once in the area, things may start to sour. Look at your dislikes for the same period. Are they all permanent ones, such as concerns over the area's high cost of living or lack of adequate housing? This may signal a much more basic concern that you should not ignore.

Don't fail to write down your likes and dislikes for at least two reasons. First, this is the only way you can spot a pattern or trend in your feelings toward the community. Second, reviewing your list weekly lets you look at what may have appeared to be an insignificant factor when you wrote it down but, on weekly review, begins to appear significant.

After your lists have grown somewhat, break them down by category (cost of living, activities, housing, climate, etc.) and review them that way. Even more trends are likely to emerge.

If you finally decide that this is where you've always wanted to retire, do so secure in the knowledge that you've done enough research and careful preparation to make certain you aren't making a mistake.

WHAT KIND OF HOUSING?

Whether you have always owned your own home or lived in an apartment, the question of where to live during retirement involves the practical determination of how much housing you want and need.

Apartment

Owning your own home is part of the American dream. But along with that dream comes not only high initial cost but care and upkeep, which can be physically demanding and expensive, particularly as property begins to age somewhat. On the other hand, living in an apartment deprives us of the feeling of living in our own property and the freedom this brings. It also deprives us of the opportunity to own an asset of considerable value which usually appreciates in inflationary times.

Yet an apartment does offer the protection of close-by neighbors, lack of responsibility for yard care and upkeep of the building, and fewer difficulties if you decide to move again than you would have in selling a house. These can be valuable advantages.

Condominium

Somewhere between the extremes of owning a house and living in an apartment owned by a landlord is purchasing a condominium. In a condominium, you own an individual living unit in a multiunit building or development.

As a condominium owner, you own your living unit outright. You also own an interest in the common area of the condominium project as a whole. You have the advantages of nearby neighbors, maintenance performed by someone else, and, quite often, security arrangements which provide additional protection. And you have the added advantage of owning the property and realizing any increase in value that occurs because of inflation. Moreover, with condominiums as well as apartments, you often have access to tennis courts, swimming pools, golf courses, and the like, which you might not be able to afford separately.

Co-op

In a cooperative, title to the real estate is owned by a corporation which issues stock to the residents/owners in proportion to each owner's interest in the co-op—usually based on floor space. The cooperative issues a lease to each resident granting them the right to possess their apartment. So, when buying a cooperative the buyer pays for the shares of stock and the right to have a lease. Monthly payments are then made to the corporation to pay for maintenance and to reduce the buildings monthly mortgage costs.

Questions You Should Ask

If you are thinking of moving into an apartment, condominium or co-op and have been living in a house over the years, there are a number of questions you must consider.

1. How much rent can you afford to pay, or how much can you afford to pay for a condominium or co-op?
2. What condition is the apartment, condominium, or co-op in, and what facilities does it offer? (See Appendix A for a checklist for evaluating an apartment, condominium or co-op.)
3. What does the lease provide? If you get serious about an apartment, you will want to have the lease reviewed by a lawyer, who can tell you whether you need to buy liability and renter's insurance or do anything special to fulfill the requirements of the lease.
4. Will you have to pay any additional money other than your rent or purchase price to secure the apartment, condominium, or co-op?
5. Is there a tenants' organization or an owners' organization? How is it run?
6. What special accommodations are available for the elderly? Are there many stairs, or is the entire facility laid out on one floor? Are the doorways wide enough to permit the passage of wheelchairs? Is the bathtub easy to get in and out of or is it a sunken one, glamorous but awkward to use? Must you climb stairs to get in from outside? Are the electrical outlets placed at least two feet above the floor so that not much stooping is required? And, finally, does the apartment or condominium strike you as the kind of place you'd like to live in for the rest of your life? (See Appendix B for a checklist of these housing considerations.)

A FINAL WORD

Aging and retiring are not all negative. As older citizens become a major economic force in the marketplace, their dollars are more sought after. Senior-citizen discounts and other economic come-ons offer significant advantages to persons over sixty-five who frequent the marketplace. From drug discounts to college-enrollment breaks to health-club rebates, businesses are going after senior citizens as high-volume, dependable customers.

Despite the rigors of old age and the uncertainties of the great change that retirement is, we may well be entering a golden age for retirees in this country. If you plan now, you can assure a retirement successful beyond your expectations.

4

Your Retirement System—The Cornerstone of Your Planning

One of the key factors for a happy retirement is having sufficient funds to live on. This may seem pretty self-evident, but it is something to think about. One recent study suggests that right now it takes a net worth of $300,000 to retire comfortably but not lavishly. And five years from now, assuming an inflation rate of 8 percent, you'll need assets of about $440,000 to retire comfortably. These figures assume that you will not spend any of the principal of your assets and will be able to live on a 10-percent return on these assets.

These figures may or may not turn out to be accurate. And in any event, they involve someone else's calculation of what you need to live comfortably in retirement. You alone can determine what your needs are and what you consider comfortable. But you must make these decisions. You must determine what your financial needs will be and what income you can expect. The difference between the income from your retirement plan, Social Security, and any other sources, and your financial needs after retirement represents additional money you will have to accumulate to prepare for retirement.

YOUR POSTRETIREMENT FINANCIAL NEEDS

The President's Commission on Pension Policy, established by President Carter, has studied the income needs of retirees and compared them with the income needs of persons still in the work force. The commission discovered that despite widespread belief to the contrary, postretirement net income needs are not substantially less than preretirement net income needs.

The following table, developed by the commission, shows the income required after retirement to maintain preretirement living standards. The calculations are based on 1980 figures.

From this table, you can see that a married couple with a gross preretirement income of $30,000 will need a postretirement income of $18,062, or about 60 percent of gross preretirement income, to maintain an equivalent standard of living. According to the most recent estimates, Social Security will provide about 40 percent of the couple's gross preretirement income. So there is a gap between retirement income needs and retirement income which must be filled from some other source.

The gap between retirement needs and retirement income is even greater with a single worker, since Social Security will provide only 30 percent of the preretirement income that the single employee would need to have equivalent retirement income.

Appendix C provides a form for determining your postretirement income needs and calculating your "income gap." Bridging this income gap is a serious problem for workers facing retirement. For about 75 percent of America's non-farm workers over the age of twenty-five, some sort of private, employer-funded pension plan is used to satisfy at least part of this need.

PRIVATE EMPLOYER-FUNDED PENSION PLANS

The idea behind a private, employer-funded pension plan is for the employee to give up certain wage or salary benefits now so that money can be paid into a fund by the employer/company to provide retirement income later. But there is a problem with this theory. If the employee gives up wage benefits now, he should be

Table 4-1
Income Required After Retirement to Maintain Preretirement Living Standard

1 Gross pre-retirement income	2 Taxes	3 Work-related expenses	4 Savings and invest-ments	5 Net pre-retirement income	6 Post-retirement income taxes	7 Equivalent retirement income	8 % of pre-retirement gross income
				(1 minus 3 & 4)		(5 plus 6)	(7 divided by 1)
				Single People			
$10,000	$ 2,008	$ 480	$ 240	$ 7,272	$———	$ 7,272	73%
15,000	3,703	678	678	9,941	———	9,941	66%
20,000	5,783	853	1,280	12,084	198	12,282	61%
30,000	10,355	1,179	2,357	16,109	1,282	17,391	58%
50,000	22,249	1,665	4,163	21,923	3,752	25,675	51%
				Married Couples			
$10,000	$ 1,444	$ 513	$ 257	$ 7,786	$———	$ 7,786	78%
15,000	2,860	728	728	10,684	———	10,684	71%
20,000	4,488	931	1,396	13,185	63	13,185	66%
30,000	8,047	1,317	2,634	17,999	63	18,062	60%
50,000	17,824	1,931	4,826	25,419	1,965	27,384	55%

assured that the retirement benefits will be there when he retires. This has not always been the case. In 1963, the Studebaker Corporation, an automobile manufacturer, closed its huge plant in South Bend, Indiana, and moved to Canada. Of the eight thousand South Bend workers, all except a few who chose to move to Canada with the company lost their pension benefits.

The Studebaker disaster led to a decade of Congressional investigation into pension-plan abuses and suggestions for how to deal with them. In 1974, Congress enacted the Employees Retirement Income Security Act, known as ERISA. ERISA established certain rights for participants in private pension plans and set up minimum standards for the operation of those plans. Among the protections afforded by ERISA are the following:

1. If your pension plan is subject to ERISA (ERISA does not cover governmental plans, church plans, excess-benefits plans, and certain other limited types of pension plans), the plan administrator must provide you with a summary of its provisions. This summary is known as a Summary Plan Description, or SPD, and it must be written in understandable language.
2. The plan administrator is also required to provide you with a Summary Annual Report, which contains information on the financial activities of the plan for that particular year. If you have difficulty obtaining information about your plan from the administrator, you should contact the nearest area office of the Labor-Management Services Administration. If you do not know the address of the nearest office, contact the United States Department of Labor, 3rd Street and Constitution Avenue, N.W., Washington, D.C. 20216.

To understand your retirement plan fully, you must understand how it is funded and distributed. This will depend on the type of plan you have. There are two basic types: defined-benefit plans and defined-contribution plans.

In a *defined-benefit plan*, the amount of your pension benefits after retirement is determined in advance, but the amount of the contributions to the plan varies, depending on projections of how many employees are to receive benefits and how much the benefits will be. Roughly two thirds of the employees covered by pension plans are in defined-benefit plans. The advantage of a defined-benefit plan is, of course, that you know in advance what the pension benefit will be.

49

In a *defined-contribution plan*, the contributions to the fund are fixed but the amount of the pension benefits is not known. The benefits received after retirement are based on the amount of money in the account at that time. Defined-contribution plans are also known as profit-sharing plans.

Integration of Private Plans with Social Security

Some pension plans are "integrated" with Social Security. An integrated plan takes into account the benefits you will receive from Social Security, and a percentage of the monthly Social Security benefit is subtracted from the pension amount. The theory is that the employer is allowed to treat up to 50 percent of the Social Security benefit as part of your retirement plan, since he has financed that contribution to Social Security. This can be particularly disadvantageous for low-income employees, because Social Security benefits represent a higher percentage of their preretirement income than they do for highly paid employees.

WHAT YOU NEED TO KNOW ABOUT YOUR PENSION PLAN

What Type of Plan?

You need to know first of all whether your pension plan is a defined-benefit plan or a defined-contribution plan and whether it is integrated with Social Security.

When Are You Covered?

Next you need to know when you are eligible to participate in the plan. That is, when are you covered? ERISA permits a company to exclude employees who have not been working for them very long or who are under the age of twenty-five. The rule is actually much more complicated than this, but you need to check with your plan administrator to determine when you are covered.

When Are You Eligible to Participate?

The most important aspect of a pension plan, however, is when you are eligible to receive benefits. When you become eligible to participate, you begin to earn pension credit, and after a certain number of years of service, all or part of your benefits become "vested." That is to say, you cannot lose these benefits even if you move to another job.

At the minimum, a plan may adopt one of three vesting schedules:

1. *Graded vesting.* Under this schedule, an employee is 25% vested after five years of service, 50% vested after ten years of service, and 100% vested after fifteen years of service.
2. *Cliff vesting.* On this schedule, an employee will be 100% vested after ten years of service. There is no vesting earlier than ten years.
3. *Rule-of-45 vesting.* Under this schedule an employee with five or more years of service is 50% vested when his age and years of service equal 45 and another 10% vested in each of the following five years. (The benefit must be 50% vested after ten years of service, at the very least.)

A fourth alternative, *class-year vesting*, is also available in certain limited circumstances. This schedule provides that each year's contribution is vested by the end of the fifth year after it is made. A 1980 contribution, for example, is 100 percent vested by 1985. This method is used only with defined-contribution plans.

Note that these are *minimum* vesting schedules. ERISA permits companies to vest benefits under more liberal rules if they wish.

How Are Years of Service Calculated?

The benefits you earn are based on the number of years you work for your employer. It is necessary, then, that you know exactly what constitutes a "year of service." Under ERISA, a year of service is any period of twelve consecutive months in which an employee has worked at least one thousand hours.

In calculating whether you have enough years of service to be vested under a pension plan, the company may disregard:

- years of service before you attained the age of 21
- periods during which you failed to contribute to a plan that required contributions by the employee
- periods in which no employee accrued benefits under the plan

In addition, the company is not required to count some years if you had a break in service. Thus if you work for a few years and then take another job and return later, under certain circumstances your earlier work for the company need not be counted as years of service. You should check your summary plan description very carefully to determine how years of service are calculated and how breaks in service are treated.

When Do Benefits Begin?

Check the normal retirement age and how much service you have accumulated. (Many pension plans have a normal retirement age of sixty-five but require a minimum of ten years of service to qualify. You need to know both.)

How Are Benefits Calculated?

The means of calculating retirement benefits vary from plan to plan. A typical plan might take the average of the last five years' annual salary, multiply that by 2 percent, and then multiply again by the number of years you have worked for the company. From this figure, depending on whether the plan is integrated, an amount equal to up to half of your expected Social Security income may be deducted. For example, assume your salary averaged $15,000 per year for the last five years. Multiply $15,000 by 2%. This gives us $300. Multiply the $300 by the number of years you worked for the company and you have the amount of your annual pension, before deduction of any integration with Social Security. In our example, if you worked for the company for thirty years, your annual pension would be $9,000.

Other plans give you a monthly benefit of a specified dollar amount per year of service. For example, if the plan gives you $25 a month per year of service and you work for twenty years, your pension would be (before deduction of any integration with Social Security) $500 a month or $6,000 a year ($25 a month times 20 years of service equals $500 monthly pension benefit).

Early Retirement and Disability Retirement

You also need to check the minimum requirement for early retirement and how the benefits of early retirement are calculated. Do the same for disability retirement.

Spousal Death Benefits

You should know about the death benefits of your spouse before retirement and after retirement.

Who Contributes to the Pension?

You will no doubt already know whether your pension is being paid for by your contributions solely or by the employer's contributions solely or by a combination of the two. If you don't know, you need to find out.

If you change employers after you have vested rights in a pension plan, the Social Security Administration will have a record of your benefits under the plan with your former employer. An employer is required to provide data to the Social Security Administration whenever an employee leaves an organization with which he has a vested retirement benefit. When you file for benefits under the Social Security Act, the administration will provide you with the information it has concerning your right to this private pension.

Statement of Benefits

Finally, you should also know that you are entitled, upon request made no more often than once a year, to a statement of the benefits you have accrued and the value of your nonforfeitable benefits or the date when your benefits will become nonforfeitable under your pension plan. You should check every two or three years to see where you stand in your pension plan.

Appendix D provides a form for evaluating your pension plan. If you carefully review your Summary Plan Description in light of the information on these past few pages and complete the form in Appendix D, you will have a fairly accurate picture of your pension rights and, more important, your projected pension income.

PENSION PLANS FOR THE SELF-EMPLOYED

Self-employed persons are permitted to establish what is known as a Keogh or HR-10 retirement plan. The plan takes its name from Representative Eugene James Keogh of New York City, who labored tirelessly for the right of self-employed persons to establish tax-saving pension plans and repeatedly introduced his bill as House Resolution Number 10.

Keogh or HR-10 plans are basically the same in their general structure as corporate retirement plans, and the idea is that an employee, by making contributions to a "tax sheltered" retirement fund, can reduce his income tax.

Note that we have changed the tone of conversation very subtly from the pension plan wherein the corporation makes contributions on your behalf to the retirement, to a pension plan wherein the employee makes his own contribution. Generally speaking, the larger corporations, in which collective bargaining is involved, will make all the contributions to a union-member employee's pension plan. But higher-paid employees, who generally are not union members, are permitted to "shelter" some of their salary from taxation by making contributions of their own to the corporate pension plan on their behalf. We will see more about this sort of tax shelter later.

With a sole proprietor, of course, all of the money being contributed to a pension plan is the sole proprietor's money. Thus his contribution to a pension plan is made as a tax shelter. For example, by contributing $10,000 a year to a Keogh retirement plan, the sole proprietor pays income tax on $10,000 less.

The secret of all pension plans is that the government, by delaying taxation of salary, is helping to fund the pension plan itself. During the years when you are earning maximum income, you can withdraw money from your salary and place it in the pension plan. This money will not be taxed now but will be taxed later, when you withdraw it from your pension plan and take it in pension benefits. Presumably, then you will be retired and in a lower tax bracket. In the meantime, of course, your money has been permitted to grow in the pension plan free of taxation.

For the average worker, however, the bulk of the pension-fund payments will be made by the employer. Here the advantage to the employee is that this contribution is not considered taxable income for him at the time the contribution is made. Thus more money can be placed in the pension plan than you could have taken outright in salary, because you would have lost some of your salary to taxation.

The important thing to remember about Keogh or HR-10 plans for the self-employed is that they are basically the same sort of plans as corporate plans. If you are an employee covered by a Keogh plan, you have the same rights under ERISA as you would have under a corporate plan. From the employee's viewpoint, the two plans are virtually identical in their protections. Moreover, if you are self-employed, the Keogh plan offers you an opportunity to obtain some of the pension advantages formerly available only to employees of corporations.

INDIVIDUAL RETIREMENT ACCOUNTS

If you are not covered by a corporate or government retirement plan (or, in certain circumstances, even if you are), you may wish to consider the private pension plan known as an Individual Retirement Account (IRA).

Persons not covered by either of the above plans may contribute up to $2,000 per year of their earned income to an IRA. This $2,000 (or whatever lesser amount you choose to contribute) is deducted from your gross income when you figure your taxes.

If you are covered by a corporate or government retirement plan, you can still contribute to an IRA. Your initial contribution will not be tax deductible, but the annual earnings on the IRA investment will not be taxable, and the account will grow tax-free.

The idea with an IRA is that the money is not taxed now while you are in a higher tax bracket but is taxed upon its withdrawal, which is assumed to be after your retirement, when you are in a lower tax bracket. In the meantime, the money grows without taxes having been deducted.

Money contributed to an IRA cannot be withdrawn without penalty until you reach the age of 59½. You may, however, keep the money in the IRA until you are 70½. Then it must be withdrawn in specific amounts based on life-expectancy tables and the total amount in your account.

Contributing to an IRA is a relatively painless way to set money aside for retirement. For example, $9.62 a week adds up to about $500 a year contributed to an IRA. Saving $19.23 a week will amount to about $1,000 a year, and saving $38.46 will amount to practically $2,000 a year.

But the IRA doesn't really cost that much. For example, if you are in the 50% tax bracket, every dollar you contribute to the IRA represents a 50-cent savings in taxes. This means that it costs you only 50 cents to place one dollar in the IRA. Thus if you are in the 50% tax bracket and save $38.46 a week to contribute to an IRA, it is actually only costing you half that much, or $19.23, because the other $19.23 represents money you would have paid in taxes anyway. It is true you will pay some tax later when you withdraw the money, but it will likely be at considerably less than the 50% rate.

The IRA is one of the truly great opportunities available to persons considering retirement. For example, if you make a $1,000 annual contribution to an IRA at 12% interest compounded annually, after ten years your account will be worth almost $20,000. If you make a $2,000 annual contribution and wait fifteen years, your account will be worth $83,500. If you are nearing retirement, say age sixty, and contribute $2,000 a year for five years, at 12% interest compounded annually you will have over $14,000 in your IRA at age sixty-five. If the investment continues to earn 12% a year, this will bring you an income of over $1,700 a year or $142 a month, without touching the principal.

The IRA, then, is an excellent way to bridge the gap between your retirement needs and your retirement income.

Where to Buy an IRA

Under the law, money invested in an IRA must be invested through a custodian or trustee who has been approved by the Internal Revenue Service. This would include a commercial bank, a mutual-savings bank or a savings-and-loan association, a credit union, a brokerage house, a mutual fund, or an insurance company.

The investment you choose will depend to some extent on the type of institution you use to invest your IRA. For example, banks, thrift institutions, and credit unions will invest your money in a certificate of deposit or regular savings account, where it will earn the usual interest rate on the type of investment selected. All IRAs at banks, savings-and-loan institutions, and credit unions are insured by the federal government for up to $100,000.

Brokerage houses offer two basic types of IRAs: *self-directed* accounts and *professionally managed* accounts. Self-directed accounts allow you to control your investment by buying and selling stocks and bonds and the like. The money in a professionally managed account goes into a package of preselected investments. Insurance companies will purchase an annuity for you, guaranteeing you an income based on your average life expectancy and the yield on the investments purchased.

Banks and savings-and-loan institutions will probably have the lowest fees of all if, indeed, they charge a fee at all. Most brokerage houses charge an annual fee plus a fee for opening the account.

About the only thing you cannot invest an IRA in is collectibles, which is defined to include works of art, antiques, metals, gems, stamps, and coins.

It is important that you make the right selection for your investment, because the difference between 10 percent and 15 percent interest per year compounded annually over twenty-five years can be an enormous sum. On the other hand, you will want to assure yourself of some safety in your IRA, because this is money you intend to use for retirement. So, depending on how speculative you are, you may want to be more or less risky and take a chance on a higher-yield investment.

As explained earlier, once you have invested in an IRA, you may not withdraw the money before you reach age 59½. However, there is nothing that says you cannot have a number of IRAs as long as your total investment in IRAs does not exceed the $2,000 annual maximum; neither is there any requirement that prevents you from switching your IRA from one account to another. The rule states that you can transfer money from one account to another as often as you like, as long as the money is not under your control. (What you do is request the trustee of the IRA to make the transfer to another trustee.) Moreover, once every twelve months, you are permitted to withdraw the money yourself and invest it in another IRA through a process known as rollover.

Wise investors are now looking at mutual-fund groups as a possible investment for IRA funds. These groups include mutual funds that invest in stocks, bonds, and the money market. They permit you to purchase one of their funds and to transfer from that fund to another in the same "family" simply by making a phone call. The idea is that if interest rates remain high, you would keep your money in a money-market fund. As interest rates start going down, you may want to lock your money in at a higher interest rate in the family's long-term corporate bond fund. Then, if the stock market takes off, you would transfer to a growth stock fund. If your timing is anywhere near right, you will have been able to maximize your return on the fund.

If you are relatively young and have considerable time before retirement, you might want to be a bit more aggressive with your investment and perhaps take more risk than if you are nearing retirement and your IRA represents an important part of your retirement income. You may even wish to invest in several funds within the family and alter the balance of your investment within the fund as the economy changes. The beauty of investing an IRA in a fund family is that you can place your money in the right fund at the right time and obtain the highest possible return.

With any investment in an IRA, be sure you know exactly what fees are involved and whether any early-withdrawal penalties attach to the fund. For example, if you invest through a savings-and-loan institution, the high rate of return offered may depend on your retaining the money with that institution for a certain period of time; withdrawal before that date may result in a substantial penalty.

Also, be careful never to place into an IRA funds you may need before you reach age 59½. This money is strictly investment money for retirement and cannot be withdrawn without heavy penalty before age 59½. Should you die owning an IRA, the money in the IRA belongs to your beneficiaries just as most other assets in your estate do.

A FINAL WORD

As we said at the beginning of this chapter, having sufficient funds to live on is one of the keys to a happy retirement. You need to know what your retirement system will provide for you in retirement benefits, and then, if necessary, you can build your own supplemental retirement system with an IRA.

5

Social Security—It's "Social," but How Much "Security"?

Social Security covers a wide range of programs, including survivor's insurance, disability insurance, hospital and medical insurance for the aged and disabled, supplemental security income, and retirement (old-age) insurance. Other federal programs providing social security include unemployment insurance, black lung benefits, and a variety of public assistance and welfare services. When most people talk about Social Security, they mean what we will be referring to in this chapter—old-age or retirement insurance and some related disability and health-care benefits.

Social Security is the basic method of providing a continuing income when ordinary family earnings are reduced or discontinued because of retirement, disability, or death. Historically, Social Security has provided the average single retired worker with benefits that equal about 30 percent of the worker's average pay for the five years preceding retirement at age sixty-five. If the retiree has a nonworking spouse, the addition of her benefit raises the couple's retirement benefit to an average of about 40 percent of preretirement pay. Social Security, then, has become a significant retirement program.

According to information provided by the Social Security Administration, nine out of ten workers (and their employers) in the United States are earning protection under Social Security; about one out of every six Americans receives Social Security benefits every month; and almost all of the nation's aged population—those age sixty-five and over—have health insurance under Medicare.

Most of us, then, have a stake in Social Security, because if we live long enough, we will likely receive some benefits from the system.

The Social Security system was born during the Great Depression as one of the most significant achievements of the New Deal. The Social Security Act was signed into law in 1935 by President Franklin Roosevelt to provide some income for aged retired workers. The law was amended in 1939, even before the first benefits were mailed out, to provide payments to the dependents of workers as well.

In addition to providing income for retired workers, the Social Security program was designed to encourage older workers to retire at age sixty-five so that room might be found in the workplace for younger persons.[1]

We've all heard this said many times, but it bears repeating: *Social Security was never meant to provide for financial independence.* Or put another way, Social Security was never designed as a total retirement plan. It was meant to avoid the type of mass destitution that occurred among the elderly during the Great Depression and was designed as a base or floor upon which

1. It is often suggested that the decision to pay benefits at age 65 was taken from the German law advocated by Chancellor Otto von Bismarck. This suggestion implies that the retirement age of 65 was an artificial age selected from a foreign law with no consideration given to American needs. Actually the Bismarck law of 1889 provided for retirement at age 70, and Bismarck was long gone from the German political scene when the Germans later reduced the retirement age to 65. The United States appears to have adopted the age of 65 from the old-age insurance programs of Great Britain as well as Germany. The selection of 65 as the Social Security retirement age was also in keeping with a number of corporate pension plans in effect at that time, such as those of General Electric, Kodak, and Standard Oil.

There is no universal retirement age. In the Soviet Union, Japan, China, Argentina, and Italy, the common retirement age is 60 for men and 55 for women. In Algeria, Egypt, France, and Syria, it is 60 for both sexes. In Belgium, Chile, England, and Poland, it is 65 for men and 60 for women. In West Germany, it is 63 for both sexes; in Sweden and Norway, 67. The highest retirement ages are in Ireland, with 68 for both sexes, and Israel, where it is 70 for men and 65 for women.

individuals were to build the remainder of their retirement structure. Social Security is an important part of the overall retirement-planning financial picture, but it was never intended to be the whole picture. More about this later.

HOW "SECURE" IS SOCIAL SECURITY?

In recent years there has been a great deal of discussion about the supposed financial difficulty of the Social Security system. That difficulty stemmed from the fact that the Old Age and Survivor's Insurance (OASI) Trust Fund ran into difficulty for several years. OASI is the largest of the Social Security trust funds and is supported by payroll taxes collected from the workers whose contributions provide cash benefits for Social Security recipients.

From time to time the trustees of the Social Security system release a report that projects the financial future of the system. The report contains projections based on "worst case" economic assumptions as well as more favorable economic assumptions. In the early 1980s one of these studies revealed that, under the worst case economic assumptions, by the end of 1983 the OASI Trust Fund would be only $19.4 billion in the black and by the end of 1984 would be $4.5 billion in the red. By the end of 1986, the projection continued, the OASI Trust Fund would be $41.3 billion in the red. Under more favorable economic projections, the OASI Trust Fund was not projected to run in the red until 1986. But even under the most attractive economic estimates, the fund was projected to be in trouble by the end of 1986.

The problem stems from the fact that our population is growing older, because of a combination of lower birth rate and increased longevity. In 1950, for example, there were sixteen workers for every person drawing benefits under the Social Security system. By 1970, that figure had shrunk to four workers for each Social Security beneficiary. Today there are three workers for each Social Security beneficiary, and by the year 2025, there will be only two workers for each. As a result, there will be an increasing burden on the workers who are paying Social Security taxes to keep the trust fund solvent for Social Security beneficiaries. The problem is further aggravated by high unemployment (which reduces the number of workers paying into the OASI Trust Fund)

61

and by indexing Social Security benefits to inflation, which leads to higher and higher Social Security payments.

So the Social Security system is going bankrupt, right? Wrong! The Social Security system is a program of the United States government, backed entirely by government taxation and revenue power. It is as unreasonable to argue that the Social Security system is going bankrupt as it would be to declare that the United States government is going bankrupt.

Even those who oppose Social Security as a "socialistic" scheme must admit that it is a system to which the government—reflecting the people's wishes—is committed. The alternative is to allow people to starve or to provide them with some other (and likewise tax-supported) form of benefits. The Social Security system has worked well here and in other countries. Former President Reagan, among others, can attest to what happens when politicians dare even to suggest that we conduct significant surgery on the system, let alone abolish it.

Following the unsettling projections of the early 1980s, the Social Security law was amended significantly to strengthen it, and today the program is on a very sound financial footing. The Social Security taxes paid in 1988 exceeded the benefits paid that year, and this is expected under present law for the next forty years, at which time a sizable reserve fund is expected to exist. So the solvency of the program extends into the twenty-first century.

In spite of these bright prospects for the system, many people are still concerned about receiving their money's worth from the program. They express doubt that they will receive as much in benefits as they paid in Social Security taxes.

The fact is that most people will receive much more in retirement benefits than they pay in taxes. And those who will not will have had a valuable package of disability and survivor's insurance protection over their working lifetimes. Their Social Security taxes will have provided life insurance protection in the form of monthly cash benefits for the eligible family members in the event they die before retirement. They will also have had disability insurance protection.

An additional important, but often unrecognized, benefit of the Social Security system is that today most younger workers do not have to worry about fully supporting their parents, thanks to the benefits their parents receive from the system. Moreover, the system is a well-run one; only about one cent of each Social Security dollar paid out is spent for administrative expenses.

Social Security benefits represent a basic or "floor" retirement system, on which retirees should build a much larger retirement income structure. But have no fear. This floor will always be there, for, among other reasons, the American political system cannot afford to allow this humane and very sensible social-welfare program to die. So stop worrying about whether Social Security is going bankrupt and start figuring how you can arrange the best possible retirement under the Social Security system.

SOCIAL SECURITY RETIREMENT BENEFITS

To recap, then: Social Security is a retirement system in which each generation of workers funds the retirement payments for the previous generation. The expectation is, of course, that later generations will support them in a similar fashion.

Participation in the Social Security system is compulsory if your job is covered by the system, and a large percentage of jobs are.[2] The tax is a payroll tax, currently amounting to 7.51% of wages, which is deducted every month from the covered worker's pay and submitted to the Social Security Trust Fund by the employer, along with a matching 7.51% of wages that is paid by the employer. (This rate is scheduled to rise to 7.65% of wages for both employee and employer in 1990.) Your share of this payroll tax is reflected on your paycheck by the initials *FICA*, which stands for Federal Insurance Contributions Act.

Self-employed people pay both the employee's percentage and the employer's percentage, which amounts to a total of 15.02% for 1988 and 1989 and will rise to 15.30% in 1990 and thereafter. For 1989 self-employed persons will receive a credit against the self-

2. Participation in Social Security is *not* compulsory if you are a priest, rabbi minister, or Christian Scientist practitioner or a member of a religious group opposed to insurance. Among the jobs not covered by the Social Security system are certain departments of the federal government with their own pension system (such as the US Postal Service), certain state or local government departments, and nonprofit organizations that have elected not to participate in the system. Moreover, working with or for your family may mean, under certain circumstances, that you are not covered by Social Security. If you work for your family, you should check with your local Social Security office to find out if you are covered.

Table 5-1

Year of Birth	Normal Retirement Age[1]
1937 or earlier	65
1938	65 and 2 months
1939	65 and 4 months
1940	65 and 6 months
1941	65 and 8 months
1942	65 and 10 months
1943-54	66
1955	66 and 2 months
1956	66 and 4 months
1957	66 and 6 months
1958	66 and 8 months
1959	66 and 10 months
1960	67

Normal retirement age is the earliest age at which unreduced retirement benefits can be received.

employment Social Security tax rate of 2.0% of self-employment income. After 1989, this credit will be replaced with deductions designed to treat the self-employed in much the same manner as employees and employers are treated for Social Security and income tax purposes under the present law.

Once an individual's earnings exceed a certain amount ($45,000 in 1988), no further taxes are deducted from his or her income. Therefore, employees earning at least $45,000 in 1988 paid a Social Security tax of $3,379.50. Self-employed persons earning at least $45,000 paid a Social Security tax of $6,759.00 (before the credit).

At this time there are no planned increases in the Social Security tax rates, but the wage base on which this tax is paid will continue to rise with inflation.

Social Security benefits are based on a workers' average yearly earnings. Retired workers and their dependent spouses may file for benefits at age sixty-two, although to acquire maximum benefits, they must be at least sixty-five. Benefits to people who retire early are reduced to take account of the longer period of time over which they will receive benefits. The amount of reduction in benefits taken by retiring early depends on the number of months benefits are received before reaching sixty-five. Starting in the year 2000, the age at which full benefits are payable will be increased in gradual steps until it reaches sixty-seven. This will affect people born in 1938 and later. Reduced benefits will still be payable at sixty-two, but the reduction will be larger than it is now. Table 5-1 gives the Social Security normal retirement age by year of birth.

At the present time reduction of benefits on retirement between age sixty-two and sixty-five is calculated at the rate of ⅝ of 1% (1/180) for each month before you reach sixty-five. If you claim Social Security benefits at age sixty-two, you will receive only 80% of what you would receive had you waited until age sixty-five. If you claim benefits beginning at age sixty-three, you will receive 86⅔% of what you would have received at age sixty-five, and if you claim Social Security benefits at age sixty-four, you will receive 93⅓% of what you would have received at age sixty-five. Note, too, that once you reach age sixty-five, your benefits are not then adjusted upward, which is to say that once you claim Social Security benefits and are paid those benefits at a lower rate, that rate is fixed. You can, however, stop collecting early benefits or return to work, in which case you can start collecting again at a higher rate when you reach sixty-five.

If, on the other hand, you decide to retire *after* age sixty-five, for each month you delay receiving retirement benefits, beginning with the month you are sixty-five and ending with the month you are seventy, you will receive an extra amount in benefits when you do retire.

The rate of this delayed retirement credit varies according to your year of birth. For some people it is only 1%, while for others it will be 8% per year. At this time, for people who reach sixty-five through 1989, their monthly benefit will be increased by 3% for each year (¼ of 1% for each month) that they do not receive a benefit. Starting for people who will reach 65 in 1990 and later, the credit will be gradually increased until it reaches 8% in 2009.

Thus, if you are eligible to retire at age 65 in 1989 and do not retire until 1994 when you reach age 70, your monthly check will be 15% higher than if you had retired at age 65 and 35% higher than if you had retired at age sixty-two.

It is, then, always to your advantage to wait until at least age sixty-five so you will be eligible for the full Social Security amount or, if possible, to wait until age 70 so you can receive the

Table 5-2

Approximate Monthly Retirement Benefits If the Worker Retires at Normal Retirement Age and Had Steady Lifetime Earnings

Worker's Age in 1988	Worker's Family	Retired Worker's Earnings in 1987							
		$10,000	$15,000	$20,000	$25,000	$30,000	$35,000	$40,000
25	Retired worker only	$618	$801	$983	$1,129	$1,214	$1,300	$1,471
	Worker and spouse[1]	927	1,201	1,474	1,693	1,821	1,950	2,206
35	Retired worker only	572	740	908	1,045	1,123	1,203	1,358
	Worker and spouse[1]	858	1,110	1,362	1,567	1,684	1,804	2,037
45	Retired worker only	523	677	831	958	1,030	1,092	1,201
	Worker and spouse[1]	784	1,015	1,246	1,437	1,545	1,638	1,801
55	Retired worker only	475	614	754	862	910	946	1,003
	Worker and spouse[1]	712	921	1,131	1,293	1,365	1,419	1,504
65	Retired worker only	425	550	675	768	797	816	838
	Worker and spouse[1]	637	825	1,012	1,152	1,195	1,224	1,257

[1]Spouse is assumed to be the same age as the worker. Spouse may qualify for a higher retirement benefit based on his or her work record.

"super" Social Security amount of 115%. Right? Wrong! Assume you are sixty-two years old and apply for early (reduced) benefits. You will receive a monthly check for three years until you reach age sixty-five, when you would otherwise have qualified for the full retirement benefit. Assume that during these three years your monthly check is $600. You will have received thirty-six checks for a total of $21,600. Had you waited until you reached age sixty-five and qualified for the full benefit, you would have received a monthly check of $750, or $150 more per month. But it would take you 144 months—twelve years—to make up for the amount you would have received during the three years between ages sixty-two and sixty-five.

Moreover, during those three years between ages sixty-two and sixty-five, you would have been *paying into social security* by means of the Social Security tax. So not only will you have lost the thirty-six Social Security retirement checks you might have received, but you would have been paying into the system instead of drawing out of it.

So if you want to retire at age sixty-two or any other age earlier than sixty-five, and if your financial situation will otherwise permit it (i.e., you do not desperately need the three years' earnings between ages 62 and 65), the fact of reduced benefits because of early retirement should not deter you from taking an early retirement. You will be seventy-seven years old before you will begin to come out on the short end of the calculation. The same principle applies to waiting until after age sixty-five to retire so as to qualify for even higher benefits. Your monthly checks will be higher, but you will receive them for a shorter period of time, so the equation actually favors early retirement.

COMPUTATION OF SOCIAL SECURITY BENEFITS

The amount of retirement benefits depends on how old you are when you apply and your *lifetime* earnings on which you paid Social Security taxes. Other earnings and other types of income are not used to figure your Social Security benefit. Benefits are calculated by the Social Security system but Table 5-2 shows typical retirement benefits payable to a worker and a spouse.

QUALIFICATION FOR SOCIAL SECURITY RETIREMENT BENEFITS

To qualify for Social Security retirement benefits (or, as the Social Security Administration terms it, to "meet insured status"), you earn "work credits" that add up over the years to give you full coverage. These credits may have been earned at any time after 1936.

All employees and self-employed people earn Social Security credits the same way. In 1988, you received one credit of coverage for each $470 of annual earnings, up to a maximum of four based on annual earnings of $1,880 or more. This includes gross wages paid and net self-employment income. The measure was $460 for 1987, $440 for 1986, $410 for 1985, $390 for 1984, $370 for 1983, $340 for 1982, $290 in 1980 and 1981, $260 in 1979, and $250 in 1978. Before 1978, you had to earn each credit during a specific quarter of the year—January through March, April through June, July through September, and October through December. In those days, an employee generally earned one quarter of coverage if he or she was paid wages of $50 or more in a calendar quarter. Self-employed people received four quarters of coverage if they had self-employment net profit of $400 or more. As you can see from Table 5-3, if you reach age sixty-two in 1989, you will need thirty-eight credits to qualify for Social Security retirement benefits. By 1991 or later, you will need ten years or forty work credits.

The work credits test is not a severe one, at least insofar as the amount of earnings covered by Social Security is concerned. Essentially the test is whether you have been paying any amount into Social Security for the minimal number of years to qualify for retirement benefits. As you can see from Table 5-3, no one is ever required to have worked more than ten years or earned more than forty work credits.

Drawing Social Security Benefits While Working

If you are under seventy years of age and go back to work, your earnings may reduce your Social Security benefits. The reason is that Social Security benefits are intended to replace, at least in part, your lost earnings. And if your earnings continue above a certain minimum, then your Social Security benefits are reduced.

Table 5-3

Work Credits for Retirement Benefits

Workers Reaching 62 in	Years Needed	Credits Needed
1979	7	28
1981	7½	30
1983	8	32
1984	8¼	33
1985	8½	34
1986	8¾	35
1987	9	36
1988	9¼	37
1989	9½	38
1990	9¾	39
1991	10	40

Under the present law, your benefits are not affected if your earnings in any one year do not exceed an amount known as the annual exemption amount. This amount for 1988 was $8,400 for people sixty-five through sixty-nine and $6,120 for people under sixty-five. These limits will increase automatically as the level of average wages continues to rise.

To the extent that your earnings exceed the annual exempt amount, the Social Administration now withholds $1 in benefits for each $2 in earnings above the limit. Workers seventy years of age and older may earn any amount of income without penalty.

Beginning in 1990, $1 in benefits will be withheld for every $3 in earnings above the limit for people sixty-five through sixty-nine. Beginning in the year 2000, the age at which this withholding rate applies will gradually increase as the normal retirement age increases.

A Valuable Loophole

It used to be that in *any month* in which you earned more than 1⁄12 of the annual exempt amount, your Social Security benefits were reduced accordingly. Thus before 1978, a retiree under age seventy-two (the age was lowered to seventy in 1983) could earn unlimited amounts of income during part of a year and still collect full Social Security benefits for any month in which his earnings did not exceed 1⁄12 of the annual exempt amount. If you were retired and earned $6,000 in March 1976, for example, and earned nothing in any other month of 1976, only your March Social Security check would be affected. Now, however, when your annual earnings for a given year exceed the annual exemption amount for that year, your Social Security checks for the remainder of the year are reduced accordingly, even though you might have no income at all during some months.

However, during the first year in which you retire, you may still use the monthly test to determine whether you are entitled to the entire Social Security retirement benefit. This is allowed so that retirement-year benefits won't be affected by paychecks received during that year from work performed before retirement. And this seemingly innocent provision can mean some money to a prospective retiree who works it right.

If you retire early in the calendar year, when you have few or no months of income from your previous job, you can earn significant sums in certain months and your Social Security checks for other months in that first year when you do not have any outside income will remain unaffected. This opens up the possibility of earning outside income in a few months of that first year of retirement with very little impact on Social Security checks for most of the year.

However, occasionally a problem comes up in determining precisely when you have retired and thus locating your precise "year of retirement." If you have ever received Social Security retirement benefits or applied for Medicare hospital benefits, the year in which you receive those benefits is your year of retirement. Therefore, you may already have had your year of retirement and used up your eligibility for the monthly-earnings test in a year when the advantage was wasted.

If you have done this and you find now that it would be advantageous to have a later year of retirement, it is possible to withdraw any past claims and repay the money. Then your retirement year will be the one in which you actually retire. This can be, however, a bit sticky and should be avoided if possible.

Income That Does Not Affect Social Security

Note that only earnings have an affect on Social Security checks. Income that is not categorized as earnings will not affect your Social Security entitlement. Among the more common types of income that are not considered earnings are:

- investment income in the form of dividends from stock (unless you are a dealer in securities)
- interest income
- Social Security income itself, other pension or retirement pay, or Veterans Administration benefits
- income from annuities or trust funds
- gain from the sale of capital assets
- gifts or inheritances
- rental income from real estate you own unless you are a real estate dealer or rent out a farm under certain circumstances (if you do rent out a farm, ask for the Social Security leaflet *Farm Rental Income ... Does It Count for Social Security?*)
- royalties you receive on or after you become 65 from patents or copyrights obtained before that time
- certain retirement payments received from a partnership if you are a retired partner and the payments are to continue for life under a written agreement which provides for payments to all the partners (or to a class or classes of them)
- withdrawals from a Keogh plan or Individual Retirement Account
- court-awarded damages
- reimbursed moving or travel expenses
- sick pay
- pay for serving on a jury

KEEPING IT ALL STRAIGHT

From time to time, it is a good idea to check on your own Social Security account to assure yourself that your earnings are being properly credited to you. To obtain such a statement, call or visit your local Social Security office. The address can be found in the telephone directory under the listing "United States Government, Social Security Administration." Ask for the preaddressed postcard called Request for Social Security Statement of Earnings, which is Form SSA-7004. Complete the form by filling in your name, address, date of birth, and Social Security number. Sign the form and mail it to the Social Security Administration, P.O. Box 57, Baltimore, Maryland 21203.

The importance of obtaining a periodic report on your own Social Security account is reflected in the Social Security Administration's notice that reminds you that entitlement to monthly benefits and Medicare will depend on your record reflecting the payments that you should have made. And the administration states that if you wait more than 3 years 3 months and 15 days after an error occurs, corrections may not be possible.

So it should be obvious from this rather frightening statement that you should check on your Social Security statement of earnings at least every three years to make sure you are being properly credited with your contributions. Incidentally, there is no longer any charge for this complete statement of earnings.

DOING BATTLE WITH THE SOCIAL SECURITY ADMINISTRATION

If you believe that you are not being paid the proper amount of monthly benefits or that any other decision made with regard to your Social Security retirement benefits is incorrect, you may appeal the decision. Briefly, there are four steps to the Social Security appeal process, and you must make your appeal within sixty days from the date you receive a notice with which you disagree. The appeal steps are:

1. You may ask for a *reconsideration* of the decision of the Social Security Administration.
2. If, after this formal reconsideration, you still disagree with Social Security, you may ask for a *hearing* before an administrative law judge in the Office of Hearings and Appeals.
3. If you disagree with the judge's decision, you may request a *review* by the Appeals Council.
4. And if you disagree with the Appeals Council decision or if the council refuses to review your case, you may engage in a *suit* in federal court.

There is no charge by the Social Security Administration for any of the appeals before the administration, although you may choose to be represented by a lawyer of your choice. (Under the Social Security rules, you may also choose to be represented by someone who is not a lawyer.) The amount of the fee charged by a lawyer or a nonlawyer representative is limited and must be approved by the Social Security Administration.

Requests for reconsideration, hearing, or Appeals Council review must be made in writing and filed with any Social Security office by you or your representative. There is a special form available for making the request, and the people at the Social Security office will assist you in completing it. A request may also be made by letter. Appeal to a federal court must be made by you personally appearing for yourself (the legal term for this is "pro se") or by a lawyer representing you. The forms for making an appeal to federal court can be obtained from the nearest office of the clerk of the United States district court for your area. Look in a major metropolitan phone book for your area under the heading "United States Government, Federal District Court, Clerk's Office."

A *reconsideration* of your claim is a complete review to determine the correctness of the original decision. It consists of a thorough examination of all the original evidence and any additional evidence which can be obtained. The review is made by persons other than those who made the original decision. The opportunity to submit additional evidence is an important right, and you have a much greater likelihood of winning your reconsideration if you are able to submit new and pertinent information regarding your claim.

If you lose a reconsideration, you have sixty days after receiving formal notice of the decision to ask for a *hearing* before an administrative law judge. A hearing before an administrative law judge consists of a review before an officer of the Social Security Administration's Office of Hearings and Appeals. The administrative law judge reviews what has gone on in the case, determines exactly what issues must be decided, and asks questions of you and your witnesses. All such testimony is under oath. You and your representative may question all the witnesses, present new evidence, and examine the evidence on which the administrative law judge's decision will be based.

Again, the opportunity to present new evidence is a vital right, and if you have any additional evidence which has not been submitted before for consideration, you should raise it at this time.

The hearing before an administrative law judge is often held in the same city as the Social Security office that handled your claim or a nearby city so that you may conveniently attend the hearing and present your case in person. You may also submit your case for decision by an administrative law judge without making a personal appearance. If you do this, the judge will base the decision on the evidence that was previously submitted plus any additional documentary evidence or statements you submit. You will receive a written copy of the judge's decision, and if you disagree with the decision, you may request a review by the Appeals Council within sixty days after you have received a notice.

Review by the Appeals Council is the final step within the Social Security Administration's internal appeals process. The Appeals Council may decide to grant your request for a review or to deny it. If your request for review is granted, you have the right to file a written statement with the Appeals Council and to request an appearance to present all arguments. When the Appeals Council has made its decision, you will receive a written copy of this decision. If you disagree, believing the decision not to be correct, or if the council refuses to review the administrative law judge's decision, you may bring suit in a federal district court within sixty days of the date of the notice of the Appeals Council's decision or denial of review.

WHEN SOCIAL SECURITY BENEFITS ARE PAID

Social Security retirement benefits are paid only for months in which all conditions of eligibility are met for the entire month. This means generally that a person who applies for benefits at age sixty-two will be paid for the first time in the month following his sixty-second birthday. The only way a person can receive retirement benefits for the month he reaches age sixty-two is if he reaches age sixty-two on the first day of that month.

Social Security retirement checks are dated the third day of the month and should arrive in the mail about that same date. If the third day falls on a Saturday, Sunday, or legal holiday, generally the check will arrive on the last banking day before the weekend or holiday. Each check is for the benefit from the previous month.

If you have not received your Social Security check by the sixth of the month, you should contact your Social Security office to determine what has happened to the check. If your check is lost or stolen, contact your Social Security office immediately and report what has happened. A lost or stolen check can be replaced, but it takes time. Therefore, checks should be deposited or cashed as soon as possible after receipt.

You can arrange to have Social Security checks deposited in a checking or savings account in a bank, savings and loan association, or similar institution under what is known as the Direct Deposit System. The advantage of Direct Deposit is that you don't have to stand in line to cash or deposit your check, your money is immediately available because it goes directly to the bank and is not sitting in your mailbox, and you needn't worry that your check will be stolen or lost.

To arrange for Direct Deposit, contact the bank, savings and loan association, or similar institution and ask for Direct Deposit Form SF-1199. Completion of the form authorizes deposits into your account, and only you or those you authorize may make withdrawals. However, you should inquire of the financial institution how it will handle the Direct Deposit of your check and whether there is a charge for the service. Once you've established the Direct Deposit, you can stop it at any time.

Your Social Security Retirement Check While You're Outside the United States

It usually takes longer to deliver checks outside the United States because of the greater distance and extra handling. If you plan to be out of the country for less than three months, you may want your checks to stay in the United States and arrange to have someone else handle the deposit for you. If you plan to stay abroad for three months or more, your checks will be mailed to your foreign address if you are a citizen of the United States or of any of the countries listed on page 76.

If you are not a citizen of the United States or of any of these fifty countries, your checks will stop automatically after you have been outside the United States for six months unless you meet certain limited conditions, which are best explained to you by the Social Security Administration.

US Treasury regulations prohibit mailing Social Security checks to anyone in nine countries: Albania, Cuba, East Berlin, East Germany, Khmer Republic (Cambodia), North Korea, North Vietnam, South Vietnam, and the People's Republic of China. You cannot receive a check while you are in any one of these countries and the check cannot be sent to anyone on your behalf. However, if you are a citizen of the United States, you can get all

Argentina	France	Norway
Austria	Gabon	Panama
Barbados	Greece	Peru
Belgium	Guyana	Philippines
Bolivia	Ireland	Poland
Brazil	Israel	Portugal
Bulgaria	Italy	San Marino
Canada	Ivory Coast	Spain
Chile	Jamaica	Sweden
Columbia	Japan	Switzerland
Costa Rica	Liechtenstein	Turkey
Cyprus	Luxembourg	United Kingdom
Czechoslovakia	Malta	Upper Volta
Denmark	Mexico	West Germany
Equador	Monaco	Yugoslavia
El Salvador	Netherlands	Zaire
Finland	Nicaragua	

your back checks once you leave that country. If you are not a United States citizen, you cannot receive your back checks. In any event, you can resume receiving your benefits after you have left the prohibited country.

MEDICARE

Medicare is really two types of insurance—hospital insurance (known as Part A) and medical insurance (known as Part B)—which help protect people sixty-five and over from the high costs of health care. (Disabled people under 65 who have been entitled to Social Security disability benefits for twenty or more consecutive months are also eligible for Medicare.)

The hospital-insurance part of Medicare helps pay the cost of inpatient hospital care and certain kinds of follow-up care. The medical-insurance part of Medicare helps pay the costs of doctor services, outpatient hospital services, and certain other medical items and services not covered by hospital insurance.

Hospital insurance is automatic at age sixty-five if you are eligible for Social Security or railroad retirement checks as a worker, dependent, or survivor. *Medical* insurance is a voluntary plan and requires payment of a monthly premium. The premium for

1989 is $31.90, of which $27.90 is the basic premium and $4 is for catastrophic protection. You cannot buy Medicare medical insurance without buying the catastrophic protection. Beginning in 1989, people who are eligible for Medicare hospital insurance for more than six full months and have federal income tax liability also pay a supplemental premium for catastrophic medical coverage. The premium rate for 1989 is $22.50 for each $150 of tax liability, with a maximum annual premium of $800 per beneficiary.

Starting January 1, 1990, changes in Medicare will limit what you must pay for physician services and medical supplies; provide new coverage for preventive breast cancer screening, respite care, and certain prescription drugs; and improve your home health benefit. An expanded prescription drug benefit will begin on January 1, 1991.

INPATIENT HOSPITAL CARE

If you need inpatient care, hospital insurance pays for unlimited approved care in a Medicare-approved hospital after you pay a single annual deductible. The deductible is $560 in 1989. If you pay the hospital deductible in December, you do not have to pay it again if you are still a patient in January or are readmitted for inpatient care during January.

Covered services include semiprivate room, meals, regular nursing services, operating and recovery room costs, hospital costs for anesthesia services, intensive care and coronary care, inpatient drugs, lab tests, X-rays, medical supplies and appliances, rehabilitation services, and preparatory services related to kidney transplant surgery.

SKILLED NURSING FACILITY CARE

If you need inpatient skilled nursing or rehabilitation services and meet certain other conditions, hospital insurance helps pay for up to 150 days per calendar year in a Medicare-certified skilled nursing facility. You are responsible for coinsurance (a share of the costs) for the first eight days of care each year. Your coinsurance share is $25.50 a day for 1989. Medicare pays all other allowable charges for up to 150 days of covered care even if you are discharged and readmitted to a skilled nursing facility more than once during the calendar year.

Covered services include semiprivate room, all meals, regular nursing services, rehabilitation services, drugs, medical supplies, and appliances.

HOME HEALTH CARE

If you are confined to your home and meet certain other conditions, hospital insurance can pay the full approved cost of home health visits from a participating home health agency. There is no limit to the number of covered visits you can have.

Covered services include part-time skilled nursing care, physical therapy, and speech therapy. If you need one or more of those services, hospital insurance also covers part-time services of home health aides, occupational therapy, medical social services, and medical supplies and equipment.

HOSPICE CARE

Under certain conditions, hospital insurance can help pay for hospice care for terminally ill beneficiaries, if the care is provided by a Medicare-certified hospice.

Special benefit periods apply to hospice care. Hospital insurance will initially pay for two ninety-day periods and one thirty-day period. If additional hospice care is required, it can be extended indefinitely. A patient must be certified as terminally ill at the beginning of each benefit period.

Covered care includes doctors' services, nursing services, medical appliances and supplies including outpatient drugs for pain relief, home health aide and homemaker services, therapies, medical social services, short-term inpatient care including respite care, and counseling.

Hospice care has no deductibles, but there are small coinsurance amounts for outpatient drugs and inpatient respite care.

MEDICAL-INSURANCE BENEFITS

Each year, as soon as you meet the annual medical-insurance deductible (which for 1989 is $75), medical insurance generally will pay 80 percent of the approved charges for covered services you receive during the rest of the year. Covered *doctors' services* include surgical services, diagnostic tests and X-rays, medical supplies furnished in a doctor's office, services of the office nurse, and drugs that are administered as part of your treatment and cannot be self-administered. Covered *outpatient hospital services* are the services you receive for diagnosis and treatment, such as care in an emergency room or outpatient clinic of a hospital.

The Social Security Administration suggests you apply for Medicare insurance three months before your birthday month to assure that your protection will start the month you reach sixty-five. When you apply for hospital insurance, you will automatically be enrolled in the medical-insurance aspect of the program unless you inform the Social Security Administration that you do not want this coverage. This is, however, some of the most inexpensive medical-insurance coverage in the country, and it is difficult to foresee circumstances under which an individual of ordinary means should decline such coverage.

Medicare provides basic protection against the high cost of illness, but it will not pay all of your health care expenses. Some of the services and supplies Medicare cannot pay for are custodial care, such as help with bathing, eating, and taking medicine; dentures and routine dental care; eyeglasses, hearing aids, and examinations to prescribe or fit them; long-term care (nursing homes); personal comfort items, such as a phone or TV in your hospital room; prescription drugs and patient medicines; and routine physical checkups and related tests.

In certain situations, Medicare can help pay for care in qualified Canadian or Mexican hospitals. Otherwise, Medicare cannot pay for hospital or medical services you receive outside of the United States.

Since Medicare can't pay for everything, you should look for a supplementary health insurance policy that has been specifically designed to start paying when Medicare stops. Be careful not to buy a policy that duplicates Medicare benefits because you'll be wasting your money. Instead, get a policy that fills the gaps. If possible, retain any company or union group health insurance you had while you were working, or get some other group coverage. Group insurance is usually significantly less expensive than comparable individual policies.

If you want information about the different types of private health insurance that you can buy to supplement Medicare coverage, ask at any Social Security office for the pamphlet *Guide to Health Insurance for People with Medicare*, or for the factsheet *Should You Buy a Supplement to Medicare?*

WHEN AND HOW TO APPLY FOR SOCIAL SECURITY

Once you decide when you want to retire, you should apply for Social Security retirement checks at least two or three months in advance of that date in order to assure that your benefits will begin when you stop working. You may apply either in person or over the telephone. Once you have been interviewed over the phone, for example, the remaining paperwork can be carried out by mail. Also, your employer's personnel office may be able to help you with your application. You will need the following documentation:

1. Your Social Security card or a record of your Social Security number.
2. Proof of your date of birth. This can be an official record of birth or a religious record registered before you or your spouse were 5 years of age. Only original records can be used. All documentation used will be returned.
3. W-2 forms for the last 2 years, or if you are self-employed, copies of your self-employment tax returns and proof of filing.
4. If you are a veteran, your military discharge or service certificate. If your spouse is also applying for benefits, he or she will need the same documentation. Also, you would be wise to have a marriage certificate available, although this is not always required. If either of you has been married before, the administration will need information about the duration of the previous marriage(s).
5. Finally, if you have eligible unmarried children, you should submit their birth certificates and a record of their Social Security numbers if available.

A FINAL WORD

You must report any event that might have an effect on your benefit check. Social Security is valuable to any worker and his or her family and must be protected. If anything occurs in your life that will affect your checks in any way, you have a legal obligation as well as a moral one to report this fact to the Social Security Administration.

6

Where There's a Will (or a Reasonable Substitute), There's a Way

The term "estate planning" is not easily defined, for it includes a wide variety of activities. But, essentially, what we are talking about when we use the term is the planning for the transfer of our property, both during our lifetime and at death, with a minimum of tax cost and in such a way that it will not result in controversy.

Traditionally the cornerstone of an estate plan has been the will, by which the owner disposed of his property on death. However, as the nature of property has changed and as the tax laws have evolved to keep pace, estate planning has taken on a more important lifetime meaning and is no longer merely planning for what will happen to our assets on our death. Now it also involves planning for the maximum use of our assets while we're still living. We will see more about the lifetime advantages of estate planning later.

THE WILL

A will, simply defined, is the legal instrument by which we dispose of our estate after death. Every state recognizes the right of the owner of property to dispose of it on death as he or she wishes. There are, as we shall see, some restrictions on how we do this, but the basic fact remains that we are permitted to do so according to our own wishes. The will, then, is the major instrument used to make this disposition.

Although the technical requirements for wills vary from state to state, it is safe to say that a *written* instrument *declared* to be a will, *signed* by the person making the will, and *witnessed* by at least two competent people, generally suffices. In some states, however, handwritten wills (the law calls them *holographic* wills) are acceptable only under certain circumstances. In a few states, under extremely limited conditions, an oral will may be used to dispose of personal property on death. (Oral wills are known as *nuncupative* wills.) Appendix E lists the requirements of the various states for a valid will and which states recognize holographic and nuncupative wills.

WHAT IF YOU DON'T HAVE A WILL?

If you die without making a will, your property will pass according to your state's laws of *descent and distribution*. Dying without a will is known as *intestacy* (you are called the *intestate*). The laws of descent and distribution are also often called the *intestate statutes*.

In other words, if you die without a will, your state legislature has written one for you in what is known as the *laws of descent and distribution* or the *intestate statutes*. This legislative will is an attempt to leave your property as you would have, had you written a will.

Since the legislature can't know precisely how you or anyone else might want to leave property, the legislative will is what we might call an averaged will. That is, it is a will that reflects what the average man would do with his estate.[1] A difficulty with such legislative wills is that there is absolutely no room for any disposition of your property in any other way than as provided by the intestate statutes. For example, in my own home state, West Virginia, the intestate laws provide that if you are survived by your

---

1. Most legislative wills are drafted from a male point of view. That is only one of their problems.

spouse alone, he or she takes everything. If, on the other hand, you are survived by your spouse and a child or children, your spouse takes one third of your personal property and your children take the remaining two thirds; your real estate goes to your children, with your spouse retaining a life interest in an undivided one third of the real estate. (A "life interest" is an interest that a person owns for life. In this example the children own *all* of the real estate, but their ownership is subject to the right of the surviving spouse to use one third of the real estate during her lifetime. When the surviving spouse dies the real estate will be owned by the children, without restriction.)

"Near-Simultaneous" Death

If you are married and childless and you and your spouse are in an automobile accident and you are killed, your spouse will inherit everything you have if you live in a state with laws like those of West Virginia. Then if your spouse should die (say within a few days because of injuries received in the same accident), your spouse's entire estate (including what was inherited from you only a few days before) will pass to your spouse's family alone, and your family will receive nothing. (Of course, your family would inherit to the exclusion of your spouse's family if the sequence of deaths were reversed.) While this problem does not exist in all states, it is a good example of one that can be completely avoided by providing a properly drawn but simple will.

The Spouse's Share

If you die a resident of West Virginia or of a state with similar laws and have no will but leave a modest estate and a wife and small children, your wife will be unable to sell any real estate which you alone owned (she doesn't inherit it on your death, remember; the kids do, subject to her lifetime interest in a third of it) without going through a bothersome and expensive court proceeding designed to protect the interests of your minor children.

It can be even worse if the kids are grown and estranged from the parents. Then they may come home and dispossess their mother of her home and take their two thirds of the personal estate, which will include two thirds of any life-insurance proceeds paid to the estate of the deceased husband/father, leaving the widow inadequate assets to live on.

In most cases, however, you and your wife will own your home in joint tenancy, which, as we shall see later, means that your wife will automatically inherit the entire home. However, if your wife should remarry and then die without making a new will, her new husband will be entitled to a life estate in one third of the home—and can claim that one third even if it means taking some of the funds your children need for their support. Moreover, your wife's second husband can also claim one third of her personal estate without regard to the needs of her children.

Personal Effects

And there is always the messy problem of dividing your personal effects among your survivors. Almost everyone has some personal assets (antique furniture, a coin collection, hunting rifles, silverware) which require special attention. If you leave them behind with no direction as to their disposition, you are only inviting your family to squabble over the property. How much better it would be to direct in your will precisely how you want these divided. Then if there is any anger, it can be directed at you, and your heirs can come to the cemetery and kick your tombstone instead of starting a family feud that could simmer for generations.

Advancements

What if you have given one child substantial help but another has not needed it? At your death should your lifetime gifts to the one child be deducted from his or her share of your intestate estate? This question brings into play the legal principle known as *advancements*. If one child has received gifts of property from the decedent parent during the parent's lifetime and another child has received nothing, the law of advancements would hold the lifetime gifts to be "advancements from the decedent's estate." Thus, the child who received the advancements would have them deducted from his or her share of the decedent's intestate estate.

For example, a parent with two children gives one child $100,000 over a period of five years. The parent dies leaving no will but an estate valued at $300,000. Should each child receive $150,000? Or should the child who received lifetime gifts now receive $100,000 and the other child $200,000—making each child's total gift from their parent (lifetime and deathtime) $200,000? No matter how the question is answered, someone may be upset. If there is no evidence otherwise, the law of advancements will hold that the first child's pre-death gift of $100,000 was an advancement from the parent's estate and he will receive only $100,000 more. The other child will receive $200,000 from the intestate estate, and the two will have been treated evenly.

If the gift of $100,000 had been made in the parent's will, and nothing had been said about the remaining $300,000 in the estate, we would not have a problem because we would know that the parent wanted one child to have $100,000 more than the other. We have no way of knowing, without a will, how the parent felt about the lifetime gifts. While the law of advancements seeks to even up gifts to your children, it often results in thwarting the real intent of the estate owner.

Guardianship

If you leave children and no spouse survives, the court will appoint a guardian for your children. The court will no doubt make an honest effort to select a person you would have been likely to choose, usually a close relative. But the selection may very well be the one person you would *least* like to have as guardian of your children. If you write a will, you can nominate the person of your choice.

Executor

Someone must manage your estate after your death, paying all the bills and collecting the debts due you. As with the guardian of your minor children, you can make this selection yourself and prevent the selection of someone you would prefer not to have control of your estate.

The Real Difference Between Testacy and Intestacy

It all boils down to this: Who writes the rules under which your estate assets will be managed and distributed and your children raised—you or the legislature of your state? (If you are content to allow your legislature to do *anything* more than is absolutely necessary, you have problems beyond the scope of this book!) All the difficulties just listed can be solved with a simple will.

REQUIREMENTS FOR A VALID WILL

Generally, to execute a valid will, you need only be of age (the required age varies from state to state; see Appendix E) and of sound mind. Soundness of mind required to execute a will is known as capacity to execute a will; you are generally considered to have the necessary capacity if it is clear that you:

- are aware that you are executing your will
- know and understand the nature and extent of your property
- know who are the natural objects of your bounty and appreciate the claims they would have upon your assets
- are capable of formulating an orderly plan for the disposition of your estate

Disinheriting Your Spouse and Children

One of the signs that you have the capacity to execute a will is that you know who the natural objects of your bounty are and appreciate their claims upon your assets. You are not required to leave your property to anyone, with one small exception: You may not disinherit your spouse completely. The various states have different provisions designed to protect the spouse from disinheritance, but all are a variation of the old English concept of "dower," which gave a wife a guaranteed interest in her husband's estate, and "curtesy," which gave a husband a similar but not identical interest in his wife's estate.

Many states require that certain other beneficiaries, usually children, be remembered in the will but not necessarily given anything. The idea is that if you mention the children, even if only to say that you are disinheriting them, you have not omitted them by mistake or oversight. Other states require that certain children be given some minimal share of your estate.

One interesting item most nonlawyers overlook is that merely disinheriting a natural heir does not necessarily keep all your property out of the heir's hands unless your estate plan adequately disposes of all of your estate. For example, if you testily state in your will, "My son James having voted for Jimmy Carter in 1976, I leave him nothing," all you have done is leave him nothing *in your will*. And if your will does not dispose of all your property, your son James will take his share of the property passing outside your will under the intestate statutes. Therefore, in disinheriting heirs (other than your spouse), you should take care that your will disposes of your entire estate in order to prevent this happening.

An example of this would be if your will disposed of your home, your car, your stamp collection, and your corporate stock but said nothing about your bank account and your mountain farm. Disinheriting James will not prevent him from taking his share of the bank account and the mountain farm, since these assets pass *outside* of your will. You could easily have resolved this problem by providing in your will that all other property not mentioned specifically should pass to some specific person or institution.

Safekeeping the Will

Once you have properly executed your will, you should place it in a safe place. (A bank's safe deposit box may or may not be a good place to store your will, depending on your state's laws. Some states seal a safe deposit box on the death of the renter of the box; others do not. If your state seals the box on death, you obviously would not want to store your will there, since the very time when it would be necessary to get to the will would be the time when the box would be sealed.) You may want to store an *unexecuted* copy of the will in a handy spot such as your nightstand drawer and tell your spouse and children that the copy is there. Across the face of this copy, write "Original will in office safe" or some other direction that will locate the original for your survivors in the event of your death. On the signature page of this copy, print the names and addresses of your witnesses so that they can be located without the difficulty of reading impossible handwriting that appears on the original will. Never execute—that is, never sign and have witnessed—more than one copy of your will! It will only make revoking your will that much more difficult should you later decide to revise your estate plan and draft a new will.

Codicils

If you decide to change some small portion of your will or to make an addition to it, you can do so by means of an instrument known as a codicil. A codicil is simply a legal document, executed with the same formality as your original will, which amends that will. A will can have as many codicils as you like, but obviously the addition of each codicil adds to the possibility of confusion when the will and codicils are submitted for probate.

Never attempt to amend your will by drawing lines through provisions and inserting new ones! In most states, with certain very limited exceptions, you will only succeed in destroying the validity of your will and the additions will be meaningless. The only safe way to amend a will is to use a codicil that is executed with the same formality as the original will. And if the change to the will is of any consequence, the will itself should be redrawn and a new one executed.

The fact is that a layperson should almost never attempt to write a will. The law of wills, like most areas of the law, is rather complicated. By trying to save a few dollars in lawyers' fees, you can completely mess up your estate plan and cost yourself and your loved ones much more in taxes and other expenses than you saved.

What Is (and Isn't) a Will

It is possible under certain circumstances for a court to contend that a document you wrote but did not identify as a will is in fact a will. Common examples of this are letters written by persons who die shortly thereafter, in which they explain very explicitly what they wanted the person receiving the letter to have from their estate. "I am dying now, Mary, and I want you to have my farm and all my books" is a typical sort of provision in a letter that might be held by a court to be a will.

But you should never depend on a court to hold any document that is not clearly a will actually to be one. In the first place, for a court to do so, there must be some sort of proceeding before the court, which is always expensive and often disruptive of family relations. Second, the court may *not* find that your document was in fact a will. So if you intend to write a will, you should very clearly state that it is one and have it properly drafted and executed.

Why Your Will May Be Totally Invalid

Under the laws of most states, certain dramatic changes in your marital status can work to revoke your will. For example, in some states, if you marry after drafting a will (unless you drafted the will with the marriage in mind), your will is invalid. So, also, if you are divorced or if your marriage is annulled, your will may be revoked by operation of law. So if you have undergone some significant change in marital status since writing your will, you should check with your lawyer to be certain that your will is still in effect and current.

LIFETIME GIFTS

Of course, there are ways to pass your property on to others besides using a will. One of the simplest ways is to give your assets away during your lifetime. As we shall see in Chapter 12 in further detail, this may involve paying a gift tax, but regardless of whether a gift tax is involved, making gifts can be an effective means of reducing the size of your gross estate for estate tax purposes and also of reducing your income tax burden.

For example, you give your adult daughter six acres of land, valued at $1,000 per acre. When that land later increases in value, the increase will belong to your daughter and not to you or your estate. If the land value later soars to $10,000 per acre, you will have effectively kept $60,000 out of your gross estate by making a gift of $6,000.

Or assume that you give your daughter $6,000 worth of corporate stock, earning $1,000 per year. If you are in the 50% income tax bracket, your tax on $1,000 will be $500, leaving you with $500 after taxes. If your daughter is in the 24% income tax bracket, her tax on $1,000 will be $240, leaving her with $760 after taxes. By giving her the $6,000 worth of stock, you have provided your family with $260 more in after-tax income. And you have also kept your estate from being increased by further income from the stock.

Elements of a Gift

Making a gift is a relatively simple matter. You only need something to give, the desire to give it to someone, acceptance of the gift by the recipient, and transfer of the gift from you to the recipient. Of course, a gift can take many other forms. The cancellation of a debt, the designation of a life-insurance beneficiary, the setting up of a trust, and the purchase of services for another's benefit are all gifts.

WAYS OF MAKING GIFTS

There are basically three ways of making a gift: outright, under a custodial statute, and in trust. An outright gift is what we normally think of when we make a gift—the transfer of some object to another person, with the four elements just mentioned being present.

One problem with outright gifts is that since they are an irrevocable transfer, you must be certain that the beneficiary of the gift is capable of managing the gift. If the beneficiary is a minor child, this can be of particular concern. To permit gifts to be made to minors without having to worry about management of the gift, most states have adopted the Uniform Gifts to Minors Act, which is a law designed as a simple, convenient, and inexpensive method of making gifts to minors.

Under this act, a custodian becomes recipient of the gift and has control of the property until the minor reaches the age of majority (18, in most states). The custodian holds and manages the property for the benefit of the minor and pays to or for the benefit of the minor as much of the property as the custodian deems advisable for the support and benefit of the beneficiary. The custodian can decide, for example, that the beneficiary should have the entire proceeds of the gift or that the entire gift be preserved intact. When the beneficiary reaches majority, the custodianship terminates and the gift is owned outright by the beneficiary.

To make a gift under the Uniform Gifts to Minors Act, the donor must register the property that is the subject of the gift in the name of an adult or a custodian.

The simplicity of giving gifts under the Uniform Gifts to Minors Act makes it an attractive way to make small gifts to minors. But one serious shortcoming is that the custodianship ends at majority, and in many instances, age eighteen or even twenty-one is considered too young for a person to take complete control of substantial amounts of money or other property.

If the beneficiary of the gift is incapable of managing it because of age or other problems or does not want the responsibility of handling the property, the legal device known as a trust may be used.

A trust is a form of ownership under which one person (known as the trustee) holds and manages property for the benefit of one or more persons (known as beneficiaries). Under the trust device, legal title is held by the trustee, while the beneficiary has what is known as the equitable title. Thus, the *benefits* of ownership (which in this case belong to the beneficiary) are separated from the *duties* of ownership, which are held by the trustee.

Types of Trusts

There are many types of trusts, but basically all trusts can be broken down into two major categories. The first is *testamentary trusts,* which are trusts created in the will of the owner of the property and which come into effect when the owner dies. These are discussed later in this chapter. The second category is *living trusts,* which are trusts created while the owner of the property is still living. Living trusts may be further divided into two categories: *revocable living trusts,* which, as the name suggests, are trusts created while the owner of the property is still living and which are freely revocable and alterable during the owner's lifetime, and *irrevocable living trusts,* which are trusts created while the owner is still living but which, once they are created, are not subject to change or revocation.

The trust is an extremely flexible way of making a gift, because the donor of the gift can control the means of enjoyment of the gift. For example, assume that you have a son whom you would like to send to medical school. You have saved $50,000 for this purpose, but you fear that if you give him the money outright, he will take off for Malibu and open the surf shop he has always dreamed of owning. What can you do?

Well, of course, you could always just send him to school and pay his school expenses as they come up, but this requires a great deal of attention and work on your part (as well as passing up some tax advantages we'll talk about later). As an alternative, you can establish a revocable living trust. You convey the $50,000 to the Gotham Bank & Trust Company as trustee and provide in the trust instrument that as long as your son is regularly enrolled in medical school, the income from the $50,000 is to be paid to him in monthly installments or to the school for his benefit. When your son graduates from school or when he is no longer regularly enrolled, the trust will terminate and the $50,000 will revert back to you.

You might place further restrictions on the trust, such as requiring that your son maintain a certain academic average while he is in medical school or providing that he is to be paid only so much of the income as is necessary to maintain him in medical school, with the remainder coming back to you.

The point is that your son will now receive income from your $50,000 *only* while he is in medical school and meeting the certain restrictions of your trust, and you are free of the responsibility of paying your son's bills and managing the $50,000—your trustee does that for you. In the meantime, should you change your mind or wish to alter the provisions of the trust, you may do so simply by either revoking the trust and creating a new one or altering the specific provisions of the trust you have created.

Or, in another example, assume that you own an apartment building and a moderate-size portfolio of stock which you have created from scratch and nurtured to its present value. You may enjoy managing the apartment building and the stock portfolio, but you recognize that the day may come when you will have neither the time nor the inclination to manage either piece of property. Moreover, it may even happen that you will be unable to manage the property, and you know your spouse would not want to manage either asset. What can you do?

You can convey the apartment building and the shares of stock to the Gotham Bank & Trust Company as trustee and provide that the income from the apartment building and the shares of stock are to be paid to you during your lifetime. Your trust can provide that you are to serve as co-trustee and continue to manage the property so long as you are able and want to. When you are no longer able to manage the property, or when you no longer care to do so, the bank can take over the job as sole trustee. All the while you can enjoy the income, whether you manage the property or not. The trust can further provide that upon your death, the income from these assets will be paid to your wife for her lifetime. At her death, the trust is to terminate and the apartment building and the stock portfolio are to be conveyed to your son. You have now provided for management and disposition of your assets during your life and after your death.

The irrevocable living trust has the same advantages as the revocable living trust except that it obviously is not revocable during your lifetime. Once you have placed the assets in the trust, it cannot be amended or revoked. The advantage of this sort of trust, as we shall see in detail later, is that you can transfer assets and income out of your estate for estate tax as well as income tax purposes.

The testamentary trust is also irrevocable, simply because your death is irrevocable. (But that, of course, is another story.)

In all its various forms, the trust device permits the owner of property to convey it away and still maintain some sort of control over the enjoyment of the property. You may, for example, convey your assets in your will to a testamentary trust and provide that the income from this trust be paid to your spouse for her lifetime and that upon her death the assets be divided among your children in equal shares. Thus you have protected your wife during her lifetime by providing her with adequate income and then have conveyed assets to the children in whatever fashion you desire.

PROTECTION OF YOUR ASSETS

One of the purposes of acquiring an estate is being able to pass on the advantages of this estate to your loved ones. But this becomes a problem if your loved ones can't manage money and are likely to fritter away any property they might have.

The Spendthrift Trust

There are a number of ways to deal with this problem. The most common is through creation of what is known as a spendthrift trust, which by its terms prohibits the beneficiary from "anticipating" or "alienating" the assets in the trust.

Anticipation occurs when the beneficiary is permitted to obtain an advance on any of the income he might later receive from the trust. For example, if a trust provides that a beneficiary is to receive income of $1,000 a month, he would anticipate the income by having the trustee pay him next year's trust income of $12,000 in advance. But to do this would allow him to run through his future support in short order. The purpose of the spendthrift trust, of course, is to protect the beneficiary from doing this very thing. So anticipation is not permitted.

Alienation occurs when a beneficiary is permitted to sell to someone else his future right to payments under the trust. Thus, for example, the beneficiary of a trust who is to receive $1,000 a month and who sells his right to $60,000 over the next five years to another party for, say, $50,000 today is said to have alienated his interest. This is prohibited under a spendthrift trust.

There is, of course, no way under a spendthrift trust to stop a beneficiary from selling his right to the income from the trust. But since the trustee is not permitted to make payments to anyone other than the beneficiary of the trust, the opportunity to sell a right under a spendthrift trust is considerably limited.

The spendthrift trust does not prevent a creditor from going after any money due him from the beneficiary *after* the money has reached the beneficiary's hands. All a spendthrift trust does is prevent the beneficiary from selling, giving away, or in any way interfering with his right to receive future payments under the trust. If a creditor of the beneficiary wishes to receive payment, he must go to the beneficiary every month for payment. This is a great deal more difficult for the creditor than permitting the beneficiary to obtain an advance from his trust and pay the debt all at once.

The spendthrift trust, which is essentially a creditor-avoidance technique, is very popular in this country but is not permitted in England. However, some states will not permit a spendthrift trust, and in those states, two other devices have been invented, the discretionary trust and the support trust.

The Discretionary Trust

In a discretionary trust, the trustee has *absolute discretion* to pay money to the beneficiary or to refuse to pay it. So the beneficiary has nothing he can convey away, by gift or sale or otherwise, until the trustee pays it over to him. Thus if you have a wife who is a poor manager of money, you could convey your estate to a trustee and give the trustee absolute discretion in the matter of whether to pay anything to your wife during her lifetime. As long as your wife lives, she will have to manage within the limits of the money paid to her by the trustee. So a trustee in whose discretion you have absolute confidence could assure that income will always be there to protect your wife.

The Support Trust

The support trust is a cousin of the spendthrift and discretionary trusts. As its name suggests, the trustee is authorized to pay to the beneficiary only what is necessary for the beneficiary's support. Thus with a support trust, you could assure that your wife would always have the necessary funds for her support but nothing further to fritter on wild investment schemes or Caribbean cruises.

A problem with both the discretionary and the support trusts is that they are purposely vague. Perhaps you would have preferred that your trustee under a discretionary trust be more lenient with regard to your wife and provide her with more income than the trustee will wish to do. But only if the wife can show that the trustee is abusing his discretion (a difficult thing to show under the law) will she be able to get past this trustee and acquire a larger amount of money. So with a discretionary trust, you must have great confidence in the trustee. And in a day and age when trustees are often organizations or institutions rather than individuals, this becomes increasingly difficult. Another problem with the support trust involves the definition of the word "support." Support for a Rockefeller, a Ford, or a Mellon will certainly be different from support for us ordinary folk.

Despite all the difficulties, however, the discretionary and support trusts offer alternatives to protect your spouse and children from their own indiscretion in those states that will not permit spendthrift trusts.

TESTAMENTARY TRUSTS

As mentioned before, a testamentary trust is one that is established by your will. The testamentary trust is a device that affords considerable flexibility in planning for the disposition of your estate. It also offers protection from undue estate taxation and protection of heirs against their own indiscretion or lack of management ability. Traditionally we think of trusts as extremely complicated and expensive devices of the very wealthy. But trusts are available to persons at all economic levels and may be useful to anyone who is nearing retirement age and beginning to plan for the disposition of assets upon death and the careful use of assets while still living.

Power of Appointment

There is one problem with a testamentary trust, however: A gift of property with income to your wife for her life, with a provision that the property pass to your children on your wife's death, is "locked in" at your death. While your wife lives, there may be great changes in the children's needs, but your assets will pass on your wife's death in accordance with the directions in your will which took effect on your death.

But there is a solution to this problem. You could leave a portion of your estate in a trust that gives your wife the income therefrom for her life and provides that on your wife's death the assets in the trust are to go to your children in such shares as your wife designates in her will. This power of your wife to designate how the trust assets from your estate shall be distributed is known as *power of appointment*.

So if you draft your will in 1985, leaving your estate in a trust with income to your wife for her life and giving her the power to appoint the trust assets on her death among your children as *she* sees fit, your wife has the opportunity to take into account changes in the children's situations between your death in, say, 1990 and her own death in the year 2000. In effect, you have given your wife the power to "rewrite" your 1985 will on her death fifteen years later and to adjust your estate plans to meet the needs of your children.

The power of appointment, then, is an authority conferred by will or other document upon a person (known as the donee or the holder of the power) to determine who is to receive the property or the income therefrom on the happening of a certain event.

There are two types of power of appointment. The *general power of appointment* is one the holder may exercise in his own favor and, for tax purposes at least, is considered to be identical with actual outright ownership of the asset involved. For example, if you leave your farm to "whomever my son shall appoint, by deed or will," you have for all practical purposes left the property to your son, since he can appoint the property to himself. If he does not appoint it to himself, he has made a gift of this property to whomever he appoints it to. A *special power of appointment,* on the other hand, is one under which the holder of the power may not appoint himself. For example, if you leave your farm to "whomever my son shall appoint, by deed or will, provided that he may not appoint it to himself, his estate, his creditors, or the creditors of his estate," you have left him nothing but the authority to direct where your farm shall go. If he doesn't appoint it to anyone, your estate still owns it. If he does appoint it, there is no way he can gain any benefit from the transaction. So having a special power of appointment is quite different from having a general power of appointment.

This distinction between general and special powers of appointment becomes important later when we discuss estate taxes, because if you convey property to someone else for his lifetime and provide that upon his death he may appoint the property to anyone except his own creditors or his own estate, then he is not considered to be the owner of the property at his death and the property is not included in his estate for tax purposes. If, on the other hand, he has a general power—that is, the power to appoint to his estate or to his creditors or to himself during his lifetime—he is considered to be the owner of the property for tax purposes.

The important thing to remember about the power of appoint-

98

ment is that it provides the owner of property with the opportunity to allow someone in whom he has complete trust to rewrite his estate plan years after his death. Especially in marriages in which one partner is much older than the other, this can be a valuable asset.

For example, if you are older than your wife, you can leave your property in trust and provide that she is to receive the income from the property during her lifetime. Your will can further provide that upon her death the property is to pass to your children in such shares as your wife appoints. After you die, your wife will have the income from your property. Should she remarry, that income will still be hers. Should she have other children, she may not appoint your property to her children by her second marriage but may only appoint the property among your children as she determines is best. So you have protected your spouse with the income and have assured that no one but your children will receive the property on your spouse's death. On the other hand, you have also given your wife the opportunity to revise your estate plan and to provide for unequal distribution of assets among your children.

One other advantage of giving this power to your wife is that her mere possession of the power is bound to keep the attention of your children. They will be more likely to continue to call on their mother and pay more attention to her than they might if they were given the property outright in your will. (This may appear crass or cynical, but it is nonetheless how human nature often functions.)

HOW TO KEEP YOUR LOVED ONES FROM FIGHTING OVER YOUR ESTATE

Few things are sadder than watching a family disintegrate after the death of the surviving parent as the children and grandchildren squabble over the assets. As pointed out earlier, one way to avoid this problem is to provide carefully in your will for the disposition of all your assets. Then if there is any anger, it can be directed at you and not among your heirs. Still, some greedy child or grandchild may decide to contest the will and try to grab a larger share of the estate.

This possibility can be avoided in many states through the use of an *in terrorem* clause in your will, which provides that any party who contests the will cannot take anything under the will. So if grandson Herman, who is to receive $4,000 under his grandpa's will, decides to contest the will and grab a larger share for himself, the very act of contesting it causes him to be cut out of the will. The law regarding *in terrorem* clauses is complicated and does not always work exactly as we might wish, but it does provide some additional protection against having family squabbles over your estate. If this is a concern for you, you should discuss the possibility of the use of an *in terrorem* clause with your lawyer.

CONTRACT TO DEVISE OR BEQUEATH

Another device that can be very helpful, particularly among aged men and women of modest means, is the contract to make a will. Most of us, whether we are wealthy or of fairly modest means, have a strong desire to keep what property we have until death. (Indeed, common sense dictates that we not part with significant portions of our estate until death. There are a number of reasons for this, but the basic one, as we discussed, is simply that ownership of property is one of the things that keeps our friends and relatives calling on us until we shuffle off this life.)

Assume that you want to be sure that you are cared for properly in your declining years and are unwilling to give up your property in advance in return for the promise of care. You might establish a trust, but unless you had sufficient property to place in the trust, it would probably not yield enough income to provide for your care.

The solution to the problem is to enter into a contract to make a will regarding such property as you have. The party contracting with you agrees, in return for your agreement to will him or her your property, to care for you until your death. In such an agreement, some friend or relative could move into your home and provide the services you might need in return for an enforceable promise from you that you will leave your home and other property to him or her. The contract will be part of the probate process should you die intestate, or can be used to contest the disposition of your property should some other confusion arise.

100

IS YOUR ESTATE PLAN OUT OF DATE?

Remember that no matter how carefully worked out your estate plan may be, situations change, and a change in your estate plan may be called for. It may be a simple modification, or the alteration may require substantial surgery. You need to reassess your situation from time to time to determine if changes are needed. Among the questions you need to ask are the following:

1. Have you married, divorced, or separated since your will was written? In some states, as noted earlier, a marriage or divorce will actually void your will.
2. Have any of your beneficiaries died, or has their financial or other status changed? Your will should provide for alternative disposition of assets in case of this. But if a major beneficiary does die before you, you should review the will with an eye to revising it to take into account the beneficiary's death. Moreover, if any beneficiary has acquired sudden wealth, had a financial crisis, or suffered death in his or her family, you may want to review the will as it relates to the bequests to that beneficiary.
3. Have you had children born or adopted?
4. Have any of your children married? Your in-laws are not considered heirs under the statutes of descent and distribution. So while you may be planning to leave your son and his wife (of whom you are very fond) a part of your estate, you should be careful to include the new daughter-in-law as an alternate heir in case your son should die before you could revise your estate plan. Otherwise it may be that your daughter-in-law will be cut out of a share in your estate.
5. Have your children presented you with grandchildren? The birth of grandchildren can result in a subtle but significant change in your estate plan. People commonly prefer that their estate be divided equally among all their children. Usually when they draft their wills, they provide that if a child is deceased, his or her share should pass on to that child's children. So if you have three children, you would want your estate divided in thirds. But assume that you have three children and child A has two children, child B has two children, and child C has three children. As long as any of your children are living, you no doubt would prefer that the estate still be divided into thirds. However, if all three of your children are deceased and only your seven grandchildren survive, it is unlikely that you

101

would want your grandchildren to share unequally in your estate.

6. Have you made any changes in your life-insurance program? The changes you may have made as a result of growing older and not requiring quite so much life insurance may necessitate changes in your estate plan.

7. Has any beneficiary of your life insurance died? Life-insurance proceeds do not pass under your will (unless your life insurance is made payable to your estate) but can pass to the heirs of your beneficiary. So, if the beneficiary of your life insurance is your spouse and your spouse has died, under the terms of her will your life insurance may return to your estate, with disastrous estate-tax consequences. Also, the death of a child who is a beneficiary under your life insurance could result in the proceeds of your life insurance passing to a grandchild, with serious guardianship responsibilities being required.

8. Are your executor and your alternate executor still able to serve?

9. Are the guardian of your children and the alternate guardian of your children still willing and able to serve? Do you still want them to serve? This is one of the most significant questions you may have to ask if you have young children.

10. Have you or your spouse inherited a large estate or in any other fashion acquired a considerable sum of money? This is, as we shall see later, essentially a question of estate taxes, but one that needs to be addressed.

11. Have you moved to another state or purchased real property in another state? The law of the state where you live controls the disposition of your personal property and the law of the state where you own real property will control the disposition of that real estate. If you have moved or if you have purchased real property outside your state of residence, you should have your will carefully reviewed to see that it complies with the law of the state that will control the disposition of the assets involved.

12. Have you suffered major financial losses recently? If you have, you may want to reconsider making specific dollar amounts of gifts to certain persons and adjusting gifts to others. For example, you may wish to forgo making large testamentary gifts to children and provide greater protection for your spouse.

13. Have your friendships changed? Relatives may have died and close friendships may have formed or may be in the process of forming which could have some impact on how you wish your estate to be distributed.

14. Have your charitable interests changed? Especially if you have moved, you may have acquired a whole new set of charitable interests, which would have some impact on how you want your estate to pass.
15. Have the tax laws changed? The passage of the Economic Recovery Tax Act of 1981, the Tax Equity and Fiscal Responsibility Act of 1982, and the Tax Reform Act of 1986 have almost required that any person who has a will should have it reviewed by an expert. If the tax laws change again (as surely they will), it will be prudent to have your estate plan reviewed again.

Singles Need Estate Plans, Too

Because they have fewer financial responsibilities than married people, single persons often ignore estate planning. Curiously, the need for a proper estate plan may be greater for a single person than for married couples, for the simple reason that the tax laws and the laws of descent and distribution are very much geared toward couples.

Estate planning is common sense. Not taking the steps to provide for an adequate estate plan can cost you a good deal of money now and can cause your friends and loved ones a great deal of grief later on.

7

Probate
(and How to Avoid It)

When a person dies, his or her assets must be inventoried, all debts paid (including taxes), all debts due the decedent collected, and a final accounting made. (Think of it as the earthly version of the balance sheet we are told St. Peter reviews with us after death.) After this final accounting has been approved by the proper authorities, the decedent's property is passed on to those persons who are entitled to take it. As a result, the property passes to them with a "clear" title—that is, there are no tax liens or other obligations affecting the ownership of the property.

To the layman (and to many lawyers), this process, which is known as probate, is slow, cumbersome, and unduly expensive. There has been a growing movement for probate reform in this country over the last few years, but it is safe to say that in most instances, probate remains unchanged as yet. (However, the reform movement continues. The National Conference of Commissioners on Uniform State Laws, a body of practicing lawyers, law professors, and judges who seek to provide simplified laws for adoption by the various states, has been working in the area of probate reform for many years and promises to offer continuing suggestions. The most recent proposal is for a means of avoiding formal probate entirely in instances in which the estate is simple—no matter what its size—and the heirs of the decedent are willing to assume responsibility for all the debts of the decedent.)

Despite its shortcomings, no responsible lawyer would suggest that probate be done away with entirely. The probate process has served us well, assuring that the decedent's assets flow smoothly (if somewhat slowly and expensively) to the proper parties, that creditors of the decedent are protected, and that debtors pay what is due the estate.

The probate process has five phases:

1. *Filing the will* with the appropriate governmental body (usually known as the probate court) and appointment of the representative of the estate (usually known as an executor or an administrator). This process is typically referred to as admission of the will to probate. If there is no will, this step consists of appointing a representative of the estate.
2. *Inventorying and appraising assets* of the estate.
3. *Paying debts* owed by the estate and *collecting debts* owed to the estate.
4. *Paying taxes,* including the federal estate tax, any state estate or inheritance tax, and the income tax return of the decedent. In large estates, the determination of the estate and inheritance tax liability is a major responsibility of the administrator or the executor and the lawyer for the estate.
5. *Distributing assets* of the estate to those who are entitled to them. This distribution takes place in accordance with the directions in the decedent's will, or if there was no will, in accordance with the laws of the state in which the decedent died or owned real property.

ADVANTAGES OF PROBATE

Despite all the bad press that the probate process has received, it is not an unmixed evil. First, having gone through the process of probate, an estate will, at least to some extent, be administered and distributed under the supervision of a competent court. Especially when there are likely to be contests over assets in the estate, this can be a valuable advantage.

Second, while the probate process can be slow and ponderous, it may offer some opportunity for the members of the decedent's family to work through their grief in a healthy fashion.

There are also advantages to probate that have to do with saving estate taxes and income taxes. Any detailed discussion of this subject would be too complicated for our purposes here, but suffice it to say that this is a consideration in larger estates in determining whether to attempt to avoid probate.

DISADVANTAGES OF PROBATE

At least numerically, the disadvantages of probate appear to outweigh the advantages. First, the probate system is often expensive, with substantial commissions paid to the representative of the estate (the executor or the administrator), attorneys' fees, and fees involved with the probate court system.

Probate also involves considerable time. The length of time required to probate an estate depends on the nature of the assets in the estate, the complexity of the disposition plan of the estate (i.e., how complex the will or other instrument distributing the assets in the estate may be), and any tax problems involved. But even relatively simple estates can take a long time to settle under most state probate systems.

The time involved is usually costly in terms of money and nerves, but it can occasionally be used to secure tax advantages for the estate and the distributees of the estate. The reason is that an estate is a separate taxpayer. As we shall see later, since our income tax is a progressive tax, the more a large income can be divided among a number of taxpayers, the lower the total tax burden will be. Thus if part of a family's income can be attributed to an estate of the decedent and taxed to that estate, it may result in substantial tax savings. Nonetheless, the delay in settling an estate through probate still must be counted as a major disadvantage.

Because an estate settlement is a matter of public record, there is often considerable publicity surrounding the details. If you have nosy neighbors who are eager to know what you own and how you distributed your estate, they need only wait until the estate is settled and all the details will be placed on the public record. This is a small matter, but in a society which values its privacy, it must be counted a disadvantage. Moreover, confidence men who prey on elderly surviving spouses often use this public information to seek their victims.

Finally, while the delay factor often helps the survivors work through their grief, it can also unnecessarily prolong the agony of dealing with the death of a loved one.

On balance, probate is often a negative aspect of the passing on of one's assets to loved ones on death. Small wonder, then, that many devices have sprung up in the law to avoid it.

HOW TO AVOID PROBATE

Joint Tenancy

Perhaps the simplest means of avoiding probate is through joint tenancy, a form of ownership in which two or more persons own title to a property together and, upon the death of one, the title to the deceased owner's share passes to the survivor. The major characteristic of a joint tenancy is this survivorship aspect. (In some states, a joint tenancy between a husband and wife is known as a *tenancy by the entirety*. The legal effect, at least insofar as avoiding probate is concerned, is identical with that of a joint tenancy.)

The advantages of joint tenancy are obvious. It is exceedingly simple and convenient. Title need only be acquired in the name of the two joint tenants and the disposition of the property upon the death of either joint tenant is automatic—it passes to the surviving joint tenant.

Joint tenancy is particularly attractive in a family setting, because it affords a sense of family unity to know that the assets of the husband and wife are owned jointly, with title automatically going to the survivor on the death of the first spouse.

However, there are a number of significant disadvantages to joint tenancy which make it most unattractive in many respects. First, a joint tenancy reduces a person's legal control over the property. Each of the joint tenants gives up the right to dispose of the property held in joint tenancy in any other fashion than that provided by the joint tenancy. For example, a husband and wife may own a piece of property in joint tenancy and one or the other may decide that his or her share should pass to the children and not to the surviving spouse. But unless the other spouse is willing to dissolve the joint tenancy, the property will automatically pass to the joint tenant / surviving spouse on death, and nothing can be done about it. As the percentage of marriages ending in divorce continues to increase in this country, this must be a major consideration in establishing joint tenancies between husband and wife.

Also, when taxes are an important consideration in planning one's estate, owning property as joint tenants does not permit either owner to take advantage of the tax laws. For example, if a husband and wife own a piece of property as joint tenants and it is determined that it would be best for estate tax purposes not to pass this property automatically from the first spouse to die to the surviving spouse, the second spouse must agree to change the form of ownership. If there are obvious tax savings, the second spouse will probably agree to do so. But if the second spouse is incapacitated or for some reason cannot agree to changing the form of ownership, the estate may have to forgo significant tax savings.

Also, the loss of control over the joint-tenancy property extends to ownership during lifetime. For example, if you hold a bank account in joint tenancy with someone else, the money belongs equally to you and your joint tenant. The other party may withdraw funds which you may have deposited.

All this points up the need for complete understanding between the two joint tenants as to the nature of the ownership and what should happen to the property. Generally speaking, most lawyers suggest that except for small pieces of property and perhaps the family home, most persons should not own significant amounts of property in joint tenancy.

The Totten Trust

The Totten trust (which takes its name from a famous case involving a person named Totten) is a deposit of money in a bank or other savings institution in the name of the depositor, in trust for a beneficiary. The trust is revocable during the depositor's lifetime, and upon the death of the depositor, the proceeds are paid to the beneficiary. The Totten trust is not subject to probate.

An advantage of the Totten trust is that the depositor can retain complete control over the account and can close out the account or change the beneficiary anytime he wishes. He need not even tell the beneficiary about the trust. (Indeed, in most instances, the

Totten trust's creator does not inform the beneficiary of the existence of the trust.) The difference between a Totten trust and a bank account held in joint tenancy with another person is that the noncontributing party has no right of withdrawal of the funds of a Totten trust during the depositor's lifetime.

The disadvantage of a Totten trust is, of course, that it applies only to bank accounts. Other types of property and money cannot be placed in a Totten trust.

The Revocable Living Trust

We will examine the revocable living trust in greater detail in the next chapter. But it is important to know that one of the principal purposes of this trust is to avoid probate. The idea, again, is that during your lifetime, you convey property to a trustee who manages the property and pays the income to you. Upon your death, this property is not considered to be part of your estate for purposes of probate. (Your trustee "owns" the property, not you.) The property is then distributed by the trustee in accordance with the terms of the trust agreement. The revocable living trust is very popular as a probate-avoidance device.

Disposition by Contract

It is possible during your lifetime to enter into a contractual arrangement providing for benefits to be paid after your death. Life insurance is a good example of such an arrangement. Unless the proceeds of a life insurance policy are specifically payable to your estate, these proceeds are not subject to probate. So it is possible to convey sums of money to a life insurance company by means of premiums and then have the substantial life insurance payout pass outside your probate estate upon death.

Another such contractual arrangement that will avoid probate is the pension plan or profit-sharing plan under which you designate who is to receive the benefits upon your death. If you designate anyone other than your estate as the beneficiary of benefits, these assets will not be subject to probate. The same rule applies to proceeds payable under a deferred-compensation contract, which is used to defer payment of salary to an employee in years in which the employee has other substantial income and is in a high tax bracket and to pay these benefits later (such as after retirement), when the employee is in a lower tax bracket. The contract of payment can provide for a beneficiary other than the estate of the decedent, and the benefits payable under this contract will likewise not be subject to probate.

Finally, certain United States securities such as savings bonds may be registered in the form of "John Smith, payable on death to Mary Smith." This is an ownership form similar to the Totten trust in that during John Smith's lifetime, he is the owner of the savings bond, but upon his death, the bond automatically goes to Mary Smith and does not go through probate.

There are, then, at least four significant devices for avoiding probate. All of them have their advantages and disadvantages, depending on, among other things, the nature of the property involved, the character and personality of the parties who own the property and who will take the property upon the death of the decedent, and the tax situation of the owner of the property. But the important thing is that the decision to use any or all of these devices is often complicated and should never be made without careful advice from experts. Form books that purport to show you how to avoid probate but fail to discuss any of the disadvantages of the various devices of doing so can lead you into making exceedingly costly mistakes; it is all too easy to choose the wrong device for the wrong purpose.

8

Living with a Revocable Living Trust

Let's assume that you own a small portfolio of corporate stocks and a four-unit apartment building. You have enjoyed managing these assets over the years and would like to continue management as long as you are capable. On the other hand, you don't want to risk losing or substantially reducing the value of either asset by poor management if you should become incapable. And you would like some "standby" management in case you simply tire of the chore.

There are several means available to provide protection in either event. The first of these is the *power of attorney*. This is a legal document which transfers authority over the management of these assets to a trusted family member or adviser. You transfer as much authority as you wish, and can revoke the power of attorney at any time. The power remains in effect during your lifetime as long as you do not revoke it or are still competent.

Since an ordinary power of attorney is revoked or extinguished by the incompetence of the grantor, this would not ordinarily be a satisfactory device in the two circumstances we discussed. But in some states, the question of your competence can be dealt with by use of a *durable power of attorney*, which specifically states that it is intended to remain in effect even though the grantor becomes incompetent. The durable power of attorney could be used only in those states where the law permits it.

One drawback of any power of attorney is that the actions of the holder of the power are not subject to regular outside supervision or control. Thus while the person who holds the power of attorney for you would have the authority to manage in your stead, no one would oversee this management.

A second such device, which can be used only in instances in which you have become incompetent, is a *court-appointed committee* or other form of *guardianship*. This is a last resort. It is the sort of thing that tears families apart, involving as it does the embarrassing necessity of having a court declare a family member incompetent to manage his own affairs.

THE REVOCABLE LIVING TRUST

A third device is the *revocable living trust,* which has been discussed briefly in the previous chapter. Using a revocable living trust in our example, you would convey your building and stocks to a trustee, such as the Gotham Bank & Trust Company, *and to yourself* as co-trustee and direct that *you* are to receive the income from these assets during your lifetime. Your trust instrument would further provide that you are to manage these assets while you are still willing and capable, thus eliminating the payment of any large management fees to the bank while you actually manage the assets. Finally, the document would provide that you could alter or revoke the trust during your lifetime while you remain competent and that on your death the trust ceases and the assets in the trust pass to your spouse.

What have you done? You have removed *legal* title from yourself and placed it with co-trustees (yourself and the bank), who hold title for your benefit personally. When you die, these assets are not part of your probate estate (you didn't own them, remember—your co-trustees did) and thus they avoid probate with all the costs and delays that are part of that system. In the meantime, you can manage your assets as co-trustee just as you would have had no trust been created. The fact that you are co-trustee of the assets at your death does not mean that you "own" these assets at death. You merely "hold" them for yourself in your alter-ego capacity of beneficiary. This is a fiction, of course, but a perfectly proper one under the law. The law is full of fictions. That is only one of its problems.

If you should later become incapable of managing these assets, your co-trustee can take over this responsibility, and your assets will continue to earn income free of any mismanagement. Or, on the other hand, you may simply tire of managing the assets or you may decide to winter in California or Florida and want your co-trustee to oversee the assets. Whatever your reasons, you have already set up the "contingency" management structure which will protect your assets when you are unable to do so for any reason. This backup management service provided by co-trustees is especially attractive to retirees who wish to travel or who merely wish to divest themselves of some of their responsibilities as they grow older.

Of course, it is not necessary that you name yourself as co-trustee or take any part in the management of the trust assets. You may name another individual or organization to serve as your trustee and forgo any involvement in the management of the property. But, especially with revocable living trusts created by relatively young persons, it is fairly common for the creator of a trust to name himself co-trustee in order to reduce the costs of the trust and to maintain personal control over the assets.

One of the problems with a revocable trust is that its revocability permits the creator to revoke it and demand the return of all the property in the possession of the trustee. Such action may well take place when the creator of the trust has become mentally incompetent to manage his affairs. Not uncommonly, the demand for the return of the property that accompanies the revocation of the trust is a result of mental confusion or aberration that has led to the conviction that the trustee and others are stealing from the creator of the trust.

As mentioned earlier, the traditional way to deal with persons of limited ability who insist on managing their affairs is by some sort of guardianship arrangement. While the name for this type of arrangement varies from state to state, the practical effects are pretty much the same: The probate or surrogate court, or whatever the equivalent court is called in the state where the individual resides, must conduct a hearing regarding the appointment of someone to handle the estate of the incompetent person. This proceeding is inevitably expensive and cumbersome, and the family is subjected to the ordeal of having an elderly family member, already disabled by senility, stroke, or some other illness, declared incompetent. Moreover, the proceeding is by law an open one and a good deal of dirty family linen is aired in public.

This problem can be avoided by the use of the revocable living trust which becomes irrevocable in case of incompetence. Such an instrument would provide that should your doctor notify your lawyer and your co-trustee in writing that you are no longer mentally capable of managing your trust properties, you are automatically removed as co-trustee, and the remaining co-trustee is to act thereafter as sole trustee. Moreover, the document should provide that in such an event, the trust becomes irrevocable.

By doing this, you assure that you can maintain control over your assets while you are still able and further assure that this control ceases whenever you are no longer capable. Moreover, you will have provided your family with a means of having you relieved of the management of your property upon your incapacity without the necessity of going through a court proceeding. Through such a provision, you can be replaced quietly as manager of your property without embarrassment to yourself or your family. And because you have provided that your lawyer is to be notified by the doctor when you are considered incompetent, you are protected against any untimely attempt by your family to replace you.

Since you have made the trust alterable and revocable during your lifetime, you can add other assets to the trust from time to time, remove assets from the trust, or change any of the instrument's provisions as you like. If, for example, you are not pleased with the Gotham Bank & Trust Company as co-trustee, you can substitute another co-trustee. The point is that you have virtually all the powers you had before creation of the trust with respect to your stocks and apartment building, and you are further protected against loss of the assets should you become incapable of managing the assets.

The Revocable Living Trust and Taxes

Note, however, that while you will not be considered the owner

114

of the trust assets (the stock and the apartment building in our example) at your death *insofar as probate is concerned,* you will be considered the owner of these assets for estate tax and income tax purposes.

Thus the one disadvantage of the revocable living trust is apparent—it does not result in any estate tax or income tax savings. To accomplish savings of these taxes, you must *irrevocably* convey away the assets (at least for a time). Still, the nontax savings of a revocable living trust, combined with the other advantages of the device, may be enough to justify using it.

Additional Disadvantages of the Revocable Living Trust

Another disadvantage of the revocable living trust is that the cost of drafting such an instrument is much greater than the cost of preparing a will. Moreover, once a living trust has been executed, it is necessary to transfer investments and other assets to the trust. In the case of real estate, this requires execution of deeds. Similar documentation may be required for other types of property. Depending on the amount of property you own, this can be a lengthy and expensive process.

Moreover, once you have conveyed your assets to a revocable living trust, it can be a bit cumbersome to manage them. This is particularly true if you have been used to dealing with the property in a straightforward or even offhand way and now face the requirement of dealing with it in a third-person fashion. This is, however, a minor disadvantage.

Advantages of the Revocable Living Trust

In addition to the savings that result from avoiding probate and the avoidance of the messy necessity of establishing incapacity, the revocable living trust also has the following advantages:

1. By creating a trust to maintain control and management of your property after death, you will have created, during your lifetime, the management team that is to handle your estate upon your death. You have, in a sense, the opportunity to preview your executor's performance of those duties. If you are disappointed with what you see, you can always amend the trust and replace

the trustee with another executor you think will do a better job.

2. Property that is owned by a minor or an incompetent person requires the appointment of a court-approved guardian. This is an expensive process, burdensome in time and generally a nuisance all around. If property is conveyed to a trust, the trustee can manage the property without all the legal restrictions and the necessity for repeated court actions required of a guardianship. However, the trustee owes the same duty to the beneficiary that a guardian would owe, and so the beneficiary has the same protections that would exist with the guardianship.

3. By holding your property in a revocable living trust and providing in that trust document for the disposition of this property on your death, you will usually avoid the sort of contest of your estate plan that is generally directed against a will. For example, the most common ground for setting aside a will is that you lacked the mental capacity to write a valid one. However, if you have transferred your property to a revocable living trust, the very fact that the document has some lifetime purpose is usually sufficient to overcome any suggestion that you didn't know what you were doing when you signed the instrument. Thus your estate plan is less likely to be upset if you have a revocable living trust rather than a simple will.

4. When the estate of a decedent which is being processed through probate has been settled, the final settlement (or final accounting, as it is often called) of the estate is filed with the clerk of the probate court and is a matter of public record. As mentioned earlier, confidence men eager to learn of widows and orphans who have money need only read the newspaper accounts of the final settlement of an estate and then go to the clerk's office and read all the details, including who received the money and how much. A living trust, however, being a private contract between the creator of the trust and the trustee, is not a matter of public record. When the trust is terminated and the assets are paid to the appropriate parties, there is a final accounting made, but that accounting is made to the beneficiaries and is not a matter of public record. And although the trustee of a living trust is required to render periodic accountings to the beneficiaries of the trust, these accountings, like the final accounting, are not matters of public record. (This opportunity for privacy is a major reason why many prominent persons choose to use the revocable living trust.)

THE POUR-OVER WILL

To complete your estate plan when you convey assets to a revocable living trust, you should still have a will, if for no other reason than to dispose of assets you have not conveyed to the trust. (And there are, as we have already seen, many other reasons to justify having a will.)

The most common type of will that is utilized with a revocable living trust is what is known as a pour-over will. In this type of will, you dispose of your specific assets as you wish and then "pour over" any other assets to the trust you have already established.

For example, let's say that you have already conveyed your stocks and apartment building to the revocable living trust mentioned earlier. Since creating this trust, you have bought a small cabin on a lake and have acquired a few shares of a money market fund. Your wife is ill and has no desire to manage any of your assets after your death.

You can provide in your revocable living trust that the trust is to continue in force on your death, with all income from the trust being paid over to your wife, and on her death, the trust is to terminate and the assets are to be divided among your children. In your will, you leave a small legacy to your secretary and a pocket watch to your nephew and convey (or "pour over") the rest of your estate to the trust you created earlier. Thus your wife will have the income, via the trust, from your stocks, apartment building, lakeside property, and money market funds until she dies. And while she will have to wait for your estate to be settled by the probate process of your state to get the income from your lakeside property and money market funds, she will have the income from your stocks and apartment building *now*, without the delay of probate.

There are, again, no tax advantages to this device, but the other advantages are significant.

A WORD OF CAUTION

The decision of whether to use a revocable living trust—or any other testamentary device or substitute—should never be made without consulting your lawyer, bank trust officer, investment adviser, and others knowledgeable in these matters. In no event should you rely on printed forms from books which purport to give advice applicable to every state. The legal fees you save by doing this will be more than offset by other losses you may incur because of oversights or mistakes that proper counsel could have avoided.

9

Taxes—In General

Plato, writing in *The Republic* over two thousand years ago, said of a tyrant: "Has he not also another object which is that they [the people] may be impoverished by payment of taxes, and thus compelled to devote themselves to their daily wants and therefore less likely to conspire against him?"

Benjamin Franklin spoke in more familiar terms in 1789 when he said: "In this world nothing is certain but death and taxes." (Even Franklin failed to notice the obvious: At least it can be said of death that, unlike taxes, it doesn't get worse every time Congress convenes.)

The subject of taxes, then, is almost certain to stir up the blood of anyone who has worked hard to acquire any assets only to see them taxed away by the government and spent on policies he may not approve of.

In this country, we have all sorts of taxes, ranging from property tax to income tax to taxes on importing and exporting goods to all sorts of taxes on transferring our assets at death. As a practical matter, we can't do much about most of the taxes other than complain to our representatives in Washington or the various state capitals. And experience has proved that to be a rather futile business. But the major taxes assessed against individuals—income tax and the various taxes aimed at the transfer of our estates during life or upon death—are by their very nature subject to some manipulation by the individual taxpayer.

119

FEDERAL INCOME TAX

The federal income tax has by far the greatest tax impact on the individual American. Although it purports to tax all income from whatever source, it exempts income from a bewildering variety of sources and provides an even more bewildering variety of deductions from income that is subject to taxation.

The income tax has been with us since 1913. It began as a modest assessment against great incomes and has developed into the single greatest source of gross revenue for our national government. It is a savagely unequal tax, despite its claims to be a progressive tax: The poor pay little or no income tax, the very wealthy pay little or no income tax, and the burden is borne by the great middle class. In truth, some of this burden is borne because members of that class fail to understand the various devices that are available to help them avoid taxation legitimately.

(Here I should point out that *avoidance* of taxation by any lawful means is perfectly proper. *Evasion* of taxes is, however, a crime. The difference is that we are permitted to do all sorts of things with our lives in order to avoid paying unnecessary taxes, but once taxes have been determined to be due the government, evading the payment of these taxes is a criminal act. For example, we are encouraged to invest in certain types of businesses in order to increase research and development in specific areas determined to be in the national interest. Such investments provide us with "tax shelters," which, as we shall see later, permit us to avoid paying tax on some of the income from these investments. But whatever income is determined to be subject to the federal income tax must be paid.)

Forty-one states and a number of cities also have income taxes. In most cases, the state and municipal income taxes are based on the federal tax. Once you have completed your federal income tax return (and have settled down and regained your ability to think rationally again), the state or local income tax forms can be completed from the information on the federal return. We will not be discussing state or local income taxes. However, as a general principle, the rules that apply to federal income tax also apply to state income tax, if for no other reason than that many state and local returns are based on the federal return. (See Appendix G for income tax rates of the fifty states and the District of Columbia.)

FEDERAL TRANSFER TAXES

The federal *estate tax* is a tax on transfers at death. The federal *gift tax* is a tax on lifetime transfers (transfers made during one's life) that complements the estate tax. Under the Tax Reform Act of 1976, the two taxes were integrated and the tax rates for lifetime and deathtime transfers are now essentially the same.

Basically, this is how it works:

You acquire a number of assets during your lifetime. If you give them away during your lifetime, you are taxed on this transfer by the gift tax. If you die owning the assets, they pass on to your heirs (if you die intestate) or your beneficiaries (if you left a will), and your estate pays the estate tax on this transfer. The Internal Revenue Service has you, dead or alive. (It's very much like the first law of bicycling, which is that no matter which way you ride, it will be uphill and against the wind.)

The critical factor in the amount of estate tax your estate will pay is, of course, the size of your estate. Similarly, the gift tax you will pay depends upon the size of the gift. As is usually the case with taxes, what you give away, either at death or during your lifetime, is for tax purposes not always what you *actually* give away. Thus when we discuss the federal estate tax and the federal gift tax in detail in Chapters 10 and 12 respectively, we will see how to reduce the taxable amount of the various lifetime and deathtime gifts and thus reduce the estate and gift taxes. The important thing to understand now is that with a number of important exceptions (such as small gifts and small estates), transfers of assets, either upon death or during your lifetime, are subject to taxation.

There is also a third type of federal transfer tax known as the *generation-skipping transfer tax*. This is a tax that seeks to prevent the use of trusts and other devices to transfer assets to your children or grandchildren and to skip the payment of an estate tax in the second generation. Here is how the generation-skipping transfer tax works:

Assume that you have an estate of $400,000 (not an unusually

121

large estate nowadays). Your spouse is gone, and you want to provide for this money to pass on to your children and grandchildren. You establish a trust and convey this $400,000 to the trust in your will, which provides that the income from that trust is to go to your children during their lifetime and that upon their death, the trust will terminate and the $400,000 will be payable over to your grandchildren. Upon your death, this $400,000 will be subject to the estate tax. The money remaining after the estate tax has been paid, say $370,000, will be placed in the trust. Your children will have the use of that money (i.e., the income from the money) during their lifetime. When they die, the $370,000 will then be payable to your grandchildren.

But there will be no estate tax due on this $370,000 upon the death of your children, because they are not passing anything over to their children. They owned nothing in this trust upon their deaths but had only the right to the income during their lifetime. Thus there was no federal estate tax payable upon the death of the children, and your grandchildren receive the $370,000 without having any estate tax deducted from it. In effect, you have skipped one generation in transferring the assets of your estate to your children and grandchildren. This is where the generation-skipping transfer tax comes in. This tax taxes the $370,000 which is passed from your trust to your grandchildren upon the death of your children as though that $370,000 had been owned outright by your children. However, there is a provision that exempts from the generation-skipping transfer tax $250,000 for each child you have. Thus if you have three children, $750,000 can pass to your grandchildren free of any generation-skipping transfer tax.

Perhaps it would be simpler to think of the generation-skipping transfer tax as an estate tax that is levied against the life estate you left to your children in your original trust document. There are some questions whether the generation-skipping transfer tax will be with us very long. But for the present at least, it is part of our tax law.

STATE TRANSFER TAXES

All the states except Nevada (which I suppose pays its expenses from taxes on the gambling business within that state) impose some sort of death tax, either an estate tax or an inheritance tax.

An *inheritance tax* is imposed upon the beneficiary of an inheritance, often with the tax rate increasing as the beneficiary is further from the deceased in relationship. For example, under typical state inheritance taxes, a spouse might be taxed at 3% on all inheritance over $50,000; a child might be taxed 5% on all inheritance over $30,000; a brother or sister might be taxed 7½% on all inheritance over $20,000; and a beneficiary who is not related to the deceased might be taxed at 10% on *all* of the share he inherits. The tax rate is applied against the inheritance of the particular individual and not against the entire estate. An inheritance tax is a tax imposed on the beneficiary's right to inherit the money.

An *estate tax*, on the other hand, is levied against the entire estate and not against various portions of it which are passed on to certain individuals. It is a tax levied on the estate's right to transfer the money. As we have already seen, the federal transfer tax at death is an estate tax. (See Appendix H for a list of inheritance and estate taxes of the fifty states and the District of Columbia.)

BEFORE-TAX DOLLARS VERSUS AFTER-TAX DOLLARS

One of the keys to acquiring wealth is to learn to think in terms of before-tax dollars versus after-tax dollars. For example, if you make a gift to someone and you are in the 50-percent tax bracket, the gift actually costs you $2 for every $1 you paid for it, simply because another dollar passes to the federal government for income taxes. (And we are, of course, overlooking the effect of state taxes and any sales tax or other hidden taxes that may pertain to the item you gave as a gift.)

Thus if you purchase a $10 book to give as a gift and you are in the 50-percent federal income tax bracket, the $10 you used to purchase the gift represents what is left after earning $20, so in effect the gift cost you $20. This is true also when you invest money. If you buy a share of stock at $10 and you have already paid tax on that money, that share of stock has really cost you $20. That is the sad, sad story of after-tax dollars. On the other hand, if you are able to purchase anything with before-tax dollars, the stated purchase price of the item is actually the true purchase price.

The difference between before-tax and after-tax dollars is one of the great advantages of pension plans. For example, if 5 percent of your income for a month is placed in a pension plan, not to be taxed to you until you retire and withdraw this money, this 5 percent will grow at a dramatically higher rate than if you had purchased a retirement plan with after-tax dollars, because more money will be going into the retirement plan initially.

Assume, for example, that your monthly income is $2,000. If 5 percent of your income, or $100 per month, is placed in your retirement fund, then at the end of the year you will have $1,200 in the fund. Assuming this $1,200 earns 10 percent income, you will have at the end of one year about $1,320 as a result of having the tax-free $100 invested for you. (You will not have exactly $1,320 at the end of the first year because not all of the $1,200 was available during the entire year, but you get the idea.) In the next and following years, the $1,320 earns interest itself and compounds annually so that over a number of years, this money has grown almost magically, without the government taking a dime of it.

Now assume that you are in the 30-percent income tax bracket. If you had to use after-tax dollars to invest in your retirement plan, you would have only $70 of that $100 to invest. (Or put another way, $143 in before-tax dollars would represent a $100 after-tax investment.) And if each year the income on this investment was itself subject to tax, then at the end of the first year, instead of $120 profit, you would have only $84 to be reinvested in your retirement fund. So the fund would grow considerably more slowly than it would with before-tax dollars.

We will spend a great deal more time with this concept in later chapters. It is one of the genuine keys to developing financial security for the future.

DEDUCTIONS VERSUS CREDITS

There are three terms that need to be understood fully before we can proceed to a more careful discussion of taxes: deductions, exemptions, and credits.

Deductions are amounts that the IRS allows you to subtract from your income in order to arrive at a figure upon which tax will be levied. A typical personal deduction is real property tax.

In calculating your income tax, you are allowed to deduct from your income any money you have paid as taxes on real property. A typical business deduction might be the cost of fuel used to manufacture products in your business. Thus if fuel costs you $5,000 a year, you are allowed to deduct $5,000 from your income to arrive at the "taxable income" on which your tax will be levied.

Exemptions are deductions you are allowed to make for the people for whose care and support you are responsible. For example, if you are married and have three children, you are permitted to deduct from your income $1,000 for each of the five of you (you, your wife, and the three children) in arriving at the figure upon which the federal income tax will be levied.

Credits, on the other hand, are amounts that directly reduce your tax burden. In another federal income tax example, you are permitted a credit against income tax due for any income tax payment you have made during the year. For example, if after all the calculations you have gone through, you finally arrive at an income tax obligation of $5,000 and you have already paid quarterly installments of $4,500, then you are credited with this $4,500 and you owe only $500. Also, if you contribute to a political campaign, half of your contribution up to a total of $50 ($100 if you are married and filing a joint return) is allowed as a credit against your tax.

Note the difference: A deduction or an exemption only serves to reduce the amount of your income before calculation of the tax. If you have $20,000 income and deductions or exemptions of $5,000, your income is reduced from $20,000 to $15,000 and then the income tax is calculated on the $15,000 figure. You do not, however, have a savings of $5,000. You merely save the taxes on $5,000.

With a credit, on the other hand, every dollar of tax credit represents a dollar of taxes saved. Credits, then, are always preferable to deductions or exemptions. Perhaps this is one reason why credits are so hard to come by and the Internal Revenue Code is full of exemptions and deductions.

DON'T LET THE IRS SCARE YOU

The Internal Revenue Service (IRS) is an agency of the United States government—just like the Social Security Administration, the Federal Aviation Administration, and the Federal Communications Commission, to name three other agencies. True, the IRS touches all of us, sometimes in scary ways. But it is still an agency of the government, which means that since the government works for us, the IRS is out there collecting taxes for us.

Therefore, no responsible citizen who is making every effort to pay the tax that is due should ever worry about the IRS. Excessive fear, among other things, makes taxpayers reluctant to claim legitimate deductions in case they'll "get into trouble with the IRS." This is absurd. There is no reason to be scared into paying more tax than you owe or to be afraid to whittle your tax bill to its legal minimum. If you are trying to cheat the government out of taxes that are legitimately due, then you have every reason to worry. Otherwise, look the IRS squarely in the eye and be prepared to do battle if necessary.

Tax cheating is, according to a study based on 1976 data, costing the Treasury (that's us, folks) up to $26 billion per year in uncollected taxes. Put another way, we could perhaps reduce our total income tax burden by about 15 percent if all the taxes due the government were collected. All of us, then, have a stake in seeing that taxes are collected by the IRS. But for our own protection, we have the responsibility to see that we pay no more tax than we legitimately owe. If you have a deduction or an exemption, claim it. If it is a close question and the law is not quite clear, claim it. If you are audited, be prepared to justify exactly why you claimed your deduction or your exemption. As long as you are obviously not trying to cheat the government, things are not likely to be too difficult for you.

If you haven't all the receipts necessary, don't worry. The IRS, despite an image to the contrary, will accept reasonable estimates in a number of areas, including cash contributions, business mileage, and the like. However, the better your records are in general, the more likely the IRS auditors are to accept an estimate based on those expenses for which you have no receipt.

Remember again that the IRS is an agency of the federal government like any other federal agency. Sometimes citizens take this agency on in court, and frequently they win. There is nothing sacred or invincible about the IRS. So don't let it scare you.

A FINAL WORD

A great deal of what we will be discussing in the next few chapters involves taxes and tax savings. It is a fundamental premise that no one ought to pay more tax than he or she owes. Indeed, there are some pretty exciting ways to avoid the payment of taxes and to accumulate considerable wealth even on a fairly low income. But it is absolutely vital to understand that our objective is *never* just to save the last penny in taxes. Anyone striving to make prudent financial plans should make every effort to save every tax dollar possible *without significantly distorting the wisest plan for his future and without doing something he absolutely does not want to do.* There are a multitude of ways to save taxes, many of them actually conflicting. And it is often better to forgo tax savings which are allowed by the Internal Revenue Code than to do things with your money that either are not what you want to do or that end up running contrary to your real plans.

Tax saving is merely one aspect of careful financial planning, and it should always remain secondary to any underlying financial objectives. You should never do anything with your money that contradicts your ultimate purposes merely because it saves taxes.

So look at the tax-saving possibilities in the next few chapters as exciting opportunities for planning, but nothing more. If your plans call for taking a different direction with your money, you are not wrong and this book right. It merely means that you have other ideas. Fine. Follow your own plan and develop the best tax-saving devices that are suitable for you.

10

The Federal Estate Tax

As explained in the preceding chapter, the federal estate tax is a tax on transfers at death. It is a progressive tax, which is to say that the larger the estate, the higher the percentage of tax that is assessed. The size of your estate is the single most important factor in determining what estate tax your estate will pay.

THE GROSS ESTATE

To determine the size of your estate, we begin with the concept of the "gross" estate, which is a listing of all the assets a decedent owned at death. One of the first questions we must ask is: What makes up the gross estate? And the answer—vastly simplified— is: Everything you own at death, and then some! The Internal Revenue Code puts it quite bluntly, stating that a decedent's gross estate includes the value at the time of death of "all property, real or personal, tangible or intangible, wherever situated." So your gross estate will include, in addition to the property you own outright, various other property interests you tend not to think of as assets in your estate, as follows.

Life insurance. Your gross estate will include amounts payable to your estate under any life insurance policies you own, unless you have taken the steps that will keep life insurance out of your gross estate. (This is discussed further in Chapter 16.)

Gifts with "strings." Your gross estate will include gifts you have made during your lifetime in which you have retained either of the following:

- the right to the income, possession, or enjoyment of the property or the power to say who will possess or enjoy the property or its income
- the power to alter, amend, revoke, or terminate the gift

These gifts are included in your gross estate under the theory that you really haven't given this property away. For example, if you create a trust in which Mary is the beneficiary but you have the right to enjoy the property for your lifetime and Mary's enjoyment only begins on your death, you obviously own the property until your death (whether you actually keep the property until death or not, since you have the right to this property until death). Also, if you create a trust with Mary as the beneficiary but reserve the right to substitute John as the beneficiary, you are considered the owner of the trust assets at death, since the right to say who will enjoy the property is one of the privileges of ownership.

Property subject to a general power of appointment. As explained in Chapter 6, it is possible for the owner of property to draft a trust so another person can have the right to say who will enjoy this property. Sometimes this right to say who will enjoy the property is considered to be the equivalent of ownership. For example, if your father conveyed property to a trust and gave you the right to say who will have the title to the property (or the income from the property) and there is no limitation on whom you can designate, you have the equivalent of ownership of the property, since you could name yourself as the owner. Under these circumstances, as we saw earlier, you are said to have a general power of appointment over the trust property. When you die, the value of any property over which you have a general power of appointment is included in your estate just as is any other property you own at death. (If you had the power to appoint anyone *except* yourself as owner of the property, you would be said to have a *special* power of appointment, and the value of this property would not be taxed to your estate.)

Pension and profit-sharing benefits. Pension and profit-sharing benefits are includable in your gross estate:

- if the proceeds are payable in a lump sum, unless you elect to forgo some very attractive income tax advantages that are otherwise available for pension and profit-sharing distributions
- if the payments are made to your estate
- if the proceeds are attributable to your contribution rather than to contributions made by your employer

Claims against others. Any claims you have outstanding against others at your death, such as for rent, interest, and dividends, are includable in your gross estate.

Social Security benefits. The Social Security lump-sum death benefit is an asset which is also included in your gross estate.

Jointly owned property. Property which you own jointly with another person (even if it is owned jointly with the right of survivorship) is included in your estate up to the amount of your fractional share.

So for estate tax purposes, your gross estate may be much larger than you think. And since the estate tax will be higher when the gross estate is larger, one of the tax goals of financial and estate planning is to keep the gross estate as low as possible when the tax collector comes around with a calculator. Much of the maneuvering in traditional estate planning revolves around this goal.

VALUATION OF PROPERTY

Generally speaking, the value of the property that is included in your gross estate is its fair market value at the date of your death. However, the law permits your executor the option of electing to value all the property in your gross estate six months after your death. If your estate holds assets that were declining in value at the time of your death, permitting the estate tax to be based on the lower values six months later allows your estate to avoid some of the sting of the declining value of the property. However, you cannot have it both ways. All assets in the estate must be valued either at the date of your death or six months after your death.

Adjusted Gross Estate

The next step in calculating your estate tax is the deduction of a number of items from your gross estate to arrive at a figure known as the *adjusted gross estate*, which more nearly reflects what you *really* owned at death. The items that are deducted include:

1. *Expenses of administration of your estate.* These are the executor's commissions, lawyers' fees, court costs, appraisers' fees, and all other expenses incurred in gathering your estate, preserving it, and passing it on to your heirs.
2. *Funeral expenses.* These include reasonable expenditures for a tombstone, monument, or mausoleum; for a burial plot and its future care; and for the transportation expenses of the person bringing your body to the place of burial.
3. *Debts.* Any debts you owed at the time of your death are deducted from your gross estate. Often the largest of these debts is the expenses of the last illness that remain unpaid at the time of your death.
4. *Mortgages and liens.* Any unpaid mortgage or other indebtedness, including interest accrued to the date of your death, upon any property in your gross estate, is allowed as a deduction from the gross estate.
5. *Unreimbursed losses from casualty or theft during the administration of the estate.* These are deductible if uncompensated for by insurance or otherwise.

What the law is saying by allowing these deductions is that some of these assets in your gross estate should not be subject to taxation on the reasonable theory that you didn't die really owning them. The money used to pay funeral expenses and administration expenses, for example, is not going to be there to pass on to anyone. Neither will the money used to pay off your debts, mortgages, and liens or the assets destroyed during administration by casualty or theft losses. So these items are deducted from the gross estate before the tax is levied.

Look at it this way: If you die leaving an estate of $1,000,000, and it costs $50,000 to bury you, and you have mortgages and liens of $150,000, and you suffer another $100,000 of casualty losses during the settlement of your estate, you have not died owning a $1,000,000 estate. Rather, you have died owning an estate of only $700,000 ($1,000,000 minus $300,000), which is all that should be subject to estate taxation.

There are two other deductions from the gross estate which are permitted as a matter of tax policy. These are deductions for transfers to charity and the marital deduction.

THE CHARITABLE DEDUCTION

Transfers to qualifying governmental, charitable, or religious organizations are deducted from the gross estate because Congress wants to encourage charitable contributions. If the transfer is outright to charity, the entire gift is deductible. If, on the other hand, the gift is of a "remainder" interest, only the value of the remainder may be deducted. (A remainder, as its name suggests, is what remains after another interest is terminated. For example, if you give your farm to your wife for life and provide that on her death your son is to have the title to the farm, your son is said to have a "remainder" in the farm.)

Let's assume you make a gift to a trust of $1,000,000 of corporate stock and provide in the trust instrument that your wife is to have the income from the stock for life. Upon her death, the stock is to go to the Salvation Army. At your death, your executor could deduct from your gross estate the value of the Salvation Army's right to have the corporate stock after your wife's death. Since the right to $1,000,000 worth of stocks sometime in the future is worth less than the right to those stocks immediately, the deduction allowed in this instance will depend upon your wife's life expectancy. If your wife is quite elderly and the Salvation Army is likely to get possession of the stocks very soon (and your wife is likely to get very little money from the fund), the charitable deduction will be higher than if your wife is young and likely to live many years.

Charitable Remainder Trust

A trust whereby an individual receives benefits for a particular period of time, after which the assets remaining in the trust pass to a charity, is known as a charitable remainder trust. The beauty of charitable remainder trusts is that they permit the owner of an estate to satisfy a desire to make a gift to charity and to reduce the amount that the Internal Revenue Service will receive.

Assume, for example, that you have a substantial estate and realize that much of it would be eaten away by the estate tax on your death. Then assume that you establish a trust in your will to provide your wife with the income from the trust for her life, and on her death the trust assets are to pass to a charity. What have you done? The value of the remainder interest which will pass to the charity on your wife's death will be deductible from your gross estate, giving the charity, in effect, a substantial portion of what the tax authorities would otherwise have taken . . . and your wife will have the income from the property during her lifetime.

Here is the way it works. If you have a net estate of $1,000,000 (after all deductions), your estate tax will be $153,000. But if you leave $200,000 to a charitable remainder trust providing for $5,000 to be paid to your sixty-two-year-old wife per year for life, $72,002 of this gift is deducted from your gross estate as a charitable deduction, and you pay a total estate tax of $124,919—$28,081 less than you would have paid otherwise. Your $200,000 gift to charity "cost" your estate only $171,919 after your estate tax saving, and your wife will still receive, if she lives as long as expected, $110,000 of this $171,919 back in annual payments of income. And think how much more kindly St. Peter will look upon you when you check in at the Pearly Gates! (You may not want to discuss the charitable tax deduction with St. Peter.)

If you want to enjoy some of this gain during your lifetime, you can make a gift to a charitable remainder trust while you are still working (and are in a high income tax bracket). Your trust could provide that you, during your life, and your wife after your death, are to receive income from the trust assets and on the death of the survivor, the trust assets are to pass to charity. You will receive an immediate income tax deduction for this gift (which puts money in your pocket now—money you would otherwise have spent for income tax payments). Moreover, on your death your estate will receive a tax deduction equal to the actuarial value of the charity's right to receive the trust property after your wife's death.

(The fair market value of the remainder interest at the time of the gift is the amount of the income tax deduction. Since no capital gains are involved, this is a good way to give away property that has increased in value. If, on the other hand, the property you want to give to charity has declined in value, you should sell the property, take a capital loss, and then give the proceeds of sale to the charitable remainder trust for the charitable deduction.)

It is important to understand that only two types of charitable trusts—the charitable remainder unitrust and the charitable remainder annuity trust—qualify for the estate tax charitable deduction.

A charitable remainder *unitrust* is one that provides for payments to a private individual or individuals based on a fixed percentage of the fair market value of the trust assets, valued annually, with the assets in the trust passing to a qualified charity on the death of the beneficiary or after a specified period of time. The unitrust is particularly attractive in times of inflation, since the fair market value (and the payout to the noncharitable beneficiary) will increase with inflation.

A charitable remainder *annuity* trust is similar except that the noncharitable beneficiaries are entitled annually to a fixed dollar amount, which must not be less than 5 percent of the trust's initial fair market value. The annuity trust is attractive in that the fixed payment never varies, even in times of economic turndown.

Charitable Lead Trust

If you have a large estate ($5 million or so), state inheritance taxes and the federal estate tax become almost confiscatory. In such circumstances, a *charitable lead trust* may be to your advantage. Under this trust, a charity receives benefits from the trust for a specified period of time, after which the trust assets revert to your family or other noncharitable individuals of your choice.

At the time of the creation of this trust (i.e., on your death), your estate will be entitled to an estate tax deduction. If $1,000,000 is left to a 10% charitable lead trust for twenty years, for example, this deduction will be $851,356. (Because the IRS tables say so.) The result will be that your estate will receive the estate tax deduction on your death, the charity will have the use of the income from the $1,000,000 for twenty years, and your family (or whomever you specify) will receive the $1,000,000 twenty years later.

A Final Word About Gifts to Charity

By encouraging gifts to charity, Congress has opened an exciting area to the careful planner. While we have been talking about large sums of money in this section, smaller estates, too, can gain, although to a lesser degree, by making gifts to charity.

THE MARITAL DEDUCTION

It seems unfair that when you die and leave your estate to your wife, it should all be subject to taxation, and then when your wife dies, all that you left her (minus what your estate paid in federal estate taxes) is once more subject to taxation. If you are roughly the same age, it is possible (indeed, even likely) that you will die within a few years of each other. And this rapid double taxation of the same assets in the same generation seems even more unfair.

In a rare show of common sense, Congress agrees and has given us what is known as the marital deduction. The marital deduction allows a deduction from the gross estate for assets passing to a decedent's surviving spouse. The effect of this is to remove all the assets that pass from a husband to a wife on the husband's death from his estate for tax purposes. (And, of course, the reverse is true: Assets that pass from a deceased wife to her husband are not included in her estate for tax purposes.)

The idea is that these assets will ultimately be taxed in full to the wife anyway, either by the gift tax if she gives the assets away during her lifetime or by the estate tax if she dies still owning the assets. Nonetheless, the opportunity to pass assets on to a surviving husband or wife can become a valuable tax-saving device.

ESTATE TAX EXEMPTION

The federal estate tax law underwent a gradual change in terms of the size of the unified credit and its corresponding exemption equivalent.

135

Table 10-1
Estate Tax Unified Credit

Year	Amount of credit	Amount of exemption equivalent
1983	$ 79,300	$275,000
1984	96,300	325,000
1985	121,800	400,000
1986	155,800	500,000
1987 and thereafter	192,800	600,000

For 1983, for example, if a gross estate exceeded $275,000, a federal estate tax return (IRS Form 706) had to be filed by the executor of the estate within nine months of the estate owner's death.

The way this works is that for 1983 the law provided a credit of $79,300 against the tax imposed in Table 10-2. Since $79,300 is the amount of estate tax that would be due on an estate of $275,000, this means, in effect, that there was no federal estate tax due on the first $275,000 of an estate, and it was not necessary to file a return for an estate below that amount.

One other change that took place in Table 10-2 over the past few years is the gradual reduction of the top estate tax bracket from its 1983 top-bracket of 70 percent down to a maximum of 50 percent by 1988.

As the amount of the estate that is exempt from federal estate tax continued to increase to its present $600,000 figure, the necessity for trying to keep the evaluation of an estate low was considerably lessened. Nonetheless, a $600,000 estate is not, in times of galloping inflation, very large. Moreover, there are still state inheritance and estate taxes to contend with. So the question of how to reduce the size of a taxable estate is still very real.

REDUCING THE TAXABLE ESTATE

There are only a handful of ways to reduce a taxable estate, but for a clever estate owner, these tax-reduction methods or some variations thereof can make an enormous difference in what passes on to heirs and loved ones and what must go to the government.

Table 10-2

Federal Estate Tax Rates

If the amount is:		Tentative tax is:			
Over	But not over	Tax	+	%	On excess over
$ 0	$ 10,000	0	18		$ 0
10,000	20,000	1,800	20		10,000
20,000	40,000	3,800	22		20,000
40,000	60,000	8,200	24		40,000
60,000	80,000	13,000	26		60,000
80,000	100,000	18,200	28		80,000
100,000	150,000	23,800	30		100,000
150,000	250,000	38,800	32		150,000
250,000	500,000	70,800	34		250,000
500,000	750,000	155,800	37		500,000
750,000	1,000,000	248,300	39		750,000
1,000,000	1,250,000	345,800	41		1,000,000
1,250,000	1,500,000	448,300	43		1,250,000
1,500,000	2,000,000	555,800	45		1,500,000
2,000,000	2,500,000	780,800	49		2,000,000
2,500,000	....	1,025,800	50		2,500,000

First, you could consume all your property during your lifetime or leave it to charity. In either event, there will be nothing in the estate to be taxed. (It is true that assets left to charity will be included in your gross estate, but the deduction that is allowed from the gross estate for contributions to charity has the same effect as if you had nothing left in your estate.) But neither of these solutions is really very practical, given the normal desire of the owner of property to pass this property on to loved ones. Indeed, one of the reasons we work to acquire property during our lifetimes is to pass on the advantages that come with the ownership of property.

Second, you can leave the property to your wife and thus shelter it from taxation by means of the marital deduction. Assuming that your marriage is sound and your estate not too vast, this is possibly the best approach, especially if your wife's estate is not likely to increase above the threshold of taxation (after 1986, above $600,000) so as to cause ruinous taxation on her death. However, the problem with the marital deduction is that property left to the wife does not *escape* taxation; taxation is merely *postponed* until the death of the wife.

Third, you can divide your estate and leave as much of it to your wife as will avoid taxation now *and* on her later death. For example, assume that you leave an estate of $1,000,000. Everything over $600,000 would be subject to taxation. If you leave this $1,000,000 to your wife, who also has a $100,000 estate of her own, none of it would be taxed now. But when she dies with a $1,100,000 estate (assuming no growth in the size of either estate), $500,000 of that estate will be subject to taxation. Here is one way you could plan your estate to avoid this result:

Since your wife already has an estate of $100,000, you leave her $500,000 of your $1,000,000 estate. None of this $500,000 will be subject to taxation on your death because of the marital deduction. When your wife dies, none of it will be subject to taxation at that time because it will be "sheltered" by the $600,000 exemption. (That is to say, the $100,000 she had from her own assets plus the $500,000 you left her comes to only $600,000, and this $600,000 will be exempt from taxation.) The other $500,000 you leave in a trust providing that your wife is to receive the income from the trust for life and that upon her death the assets are to pass to your daughter. So your wife will have the benefit and use of the $500,000 you placed in trust (and you can even provide some limited means for her to get at the principal should it become necessary under certain conditions), but when she dies, this $500,000 will not be taxable to her estate because it is not *in* her estate. She had only a life interest in this property. This property was part of your taxable estate on your death. However, since this $500,000 was less than the $600,000 estate exemption after 1986, none of it was taxed to your estate, either. So you have managed to leave an entire $1,000,000 estate to your daughter and your wife without incurring any estate tax liability.

It is this combination of trust ownership (you can have the benefit of property but do not "own" it for tax purposes) and outright ownership that forms the core of modern estate planning.

The federal estate tax, then, is a tax that particularly lends itself to careful planning and foresight. Properly done, this planning can result in avoidance of the entire estate tax—or at least a considerable reduction of the tax your estate must pay.

11

The Federal Income Tax

WHAT IS "INCOME"
AND—MORE IMPORTANT—WHAT IS NOT?

To determine how much income tax you will owe, you begin with the concept of *gross income*. And just as "gross estate" is defined in all-inclusive terms in the estate-tax section of the Internal Revenue Code, so "gross income" is defined in one all-inclusive sentence: "Gross income means all income from whatever source derived, including (but not limited to) the following items:..." If this grandly broad definition were all that there was to the Internal Revenue Code, it would be simple enough. But the next six thousand pages of the code consist, in large part, of backing away from the all-inclusiveness of this one sentence.

Note, too, that this definition says nothing about the form of the income. That is, income doesn't have to be in cash or tangible personal property or any special form. Thus if someone agrees, in return for your helping him dig a ditch on his property, to mow your yard for six consecutive weeks, the value of those six yard mowings is income to you. (Whether it is traceable and whether you are actually going to have to pay tax on it is quite another question. The point is it *is* income to you and subject to taxation.)

On the other hand, there are several items that would ordinarily be considered income but are specifically excluded from gross income. These exclusions are generally not very helpful, especially to those who are nearing retirement age. For example, all the income of an enlisted man serving in a combat zone is excluded from income tax, and the first $500 per month of an officer's pay is likewise exempt. Scholarships from educational organizations are also exempt from taxation under certain circumstances, as are damages received due to personal injuries. As you can see, none of these "specificaly excluded" sources of income is very helpful except in unusual circumstances.

Adjusted Gross Income

The computation required to arrive at the amount of income tax you owe is very similar to the one used to determine your estate tax liability. We start out with gross income and then are allowed to subtract a number of deductions to arrive at a figure known as *adjusted gross income.*

As we saw on pages 124-125, deductions are different from credits and exemptions, but they all help in reducing the tax burden. Deductions can be grouped into two major categories: business and personal. Business deductions can be further categorized as employee business deductions and employer business deductions. Both types of business deductions are for expenses that represent the cost of doing business. Employee deductions are quite limited by law, for reasons known only to Congress and the IRS (and perhaps to God, if He has a tax lawyer on His staff). An employee may only deduct from gross income amounts spent for transportation, expenses while "away from home," and moving expenses, to the extent that they exceed 2 percent of adjusted gross income. Similarly, an outside salesman may deduct all expenses that exceed 2 percent of adjusted gross income. Beyond this, an employee may not deduct any other business expenses. However, an employer can deduct all the "ordinary and necessary" expenses of carrying on business or trade.

BUSINESS DEDUCTIONS

So we have the first real tax-saving opportunity for a person who is thinking about retirement: the tax shelter known as your own trade or business. As a general rule (and as with most general rules, there are probably more exceptions to this rule than there are examples that support it), you may deduct from your trade or business income all the costs of the trade or business. But you may not use your trade or business to show a loss and deduct those expenses from your ordinary income.

What that means is this: You may not open a photographic studio just because you enjoy photography as a hobby, then fail to pursue your business "seriously," show a net loss of $1,000 a year over the next five years, and deduct that $1,000 loss per year from your income at the XYZ Manufacturing Company. You may deduct all the expenses from the photographic studio "business" to the extent that they are offset by income from that business. But you may not use this business to shelter from taxation some of your ordinary income from your usual job.

So what's the break? The break is that you may use the trade or business deduction to offset income from a hobby you are developing as a retirement business. Assume, again, that you are interested in photography and think it might be fun to have a little retirement business taking photographs at weddings and the like. You can deduct from the income of your sideline photographic business any expenses of running that business up to the amount of income you received from it. Then as you near retirement, you can begin to build up your stock of supplies and equipment for the business. As your business income increases, you use these expenses to reduce the tax on your business income. You can also deduct as ordinary and necessary expenses of the photographic business the cost of the photography magazines you have been receiving all along and paying for with after-tax dollars. Also, under *very limited circumstances*, you can depreciate part of your house for your photographic studio. business. Then when you retire, your business will be ready to run at full steam, and you'll have sheltered some of the income you've earned over the years through ordinary and necessary business deductions.

Obviously your photographic business might be so successful that you simply will not have enough expenses to offset all the income. Well, that's the kind of problem you want to have, and we'll look into other possibilities for reducing that income later.

The important point to understand now is that owning a small business on the side (assuming it is a true business and not merely a write-off gimmick) will afford you an opportunity to claim certain expenses you otherwise might not be able to deduct. For example, if you want to buy a $1,000 camera and are in the

141

28-percent income tax bracket, the $1,000 you pay for the camera is what is left after earning $1,389. However, if you can have your photographic business to use as a write-off, you can buy your $1,000 camera and use this expenditure to offset $1,000 worth of income from the business. Now, instead of costing you the equivalent of $1,389, the camera has actually cost you $720, because the $1,000 you earned from the business would ordinarily have cost you $280 in taxes. By buying the camera, you save the $280 in taxes. So employer business deductions are not merely for the rich. In fact, in some respects, they do more for the middle class than for the very rich.

PERSONAL DEDUCTIONS

Once you have deducted your employee or employer business deductions from gross income, you end up with a figure known as adjusted gross income. From adjusted gross income, you subtract your personal deductions to arrive at taxable income, or the figure upon which you are taxed. Here, as in the estate tax area, the name of the game is to get the taxable-income figure as low as possible before you have to throw the calculator into gear and calculate how much you owe the government.

Standard Deduction

There are two ways to reduce the adjusted gross income using personal deductions. One is known as the *standard deduction*. The standard deduction is a flat amount of money by which your gross income is automatically reduced when you are calculating your tax. The idea is that you have certain living expenses that Congress believes should be deductible from adjusted gross income to arrive at a taxable income, such as medical bills, taxes paid to state and local communities, contributions to church, and the like. These are automatically calculated as standard amounts based on your filing status (single person, head of a household, or married filing jointly) and your income level.

For example, if you are married and filing a joint return or are a qualifying widow or widower with a dependent child, your stan-

142

dard deduction for 1988 is $5,000. You do not need to prove that you had expenses of $5,000 to deduct this amount but may deduct it automatically. If you are married and filing a separate return, the 1988 amount is $2,500. If you are single, the standard deduction is $3,000, and if you are head of a household, the amount is $4,400. Depending on how you file, the appropriate amount is permitted as a standard deduction. Beginning in 1989, all of the standard deductions will be adjusted for inflation.

Itemized Deductions

The second way to reduce adjusted gross income by means of personal deductions is by using *itemized deductions.* Congress has provided for deduction of personal expenses in six specific areas: medical and dental expenses, taxes, interest, contributions, casualty or theft loss(es), and miscellaneous. Here is where the game of "reduce your own tax burden" begins in earnest!

Assuming you have kept accurate records to justify most of your expenditures (a simple canceled check will do), you are permitted to deduct the following:

- unreimbursed *medical and dental expenses,* to the extent that such expenses exceed 7.5% of adjusted gross income. Although prior years' medical expenses are generally deductible in the year paid, advance payments generally are not.
- *all your state and municipal income taxes; state, local, or foreign real property taxes; state or local personal property taxes; and any other nonfederal taxes you pay in the course of a year.* The deduction for taxes is only allowed for the year in which the taxes are paid or accrued. If you are on the cash basis (as most of us are), you may deduct taxes in the year in which they were paid, regardless of when they were due.
- *interest paid on the mortgage for your principal residence.* "Principal residence" is defined as your principal residence AND one other residence that you use for the greater of fourteen days or 10 percent of the days it is rented.
- *"personal" interest paid,* subject to a five-year phase-in period (beginning in 1987), after which personal interest will not be deductible. The phase-in provides that for 1987 only 65% of the deduction for otherwise deductible personal interest is allowed. The amount allowed as a deduction decreases to 40% for 1988, 20% for 1989, 10%

for 1990, and 0% for 1991 and thereafter. Personal interest is defined (vastly simplified) as interest other than interest incurred in connection with the conduct of a trade or business. In order to be deductible, personal interest must pertain to YOUR debt and must result from a genuine, enforceable, debtor-creditor relationship. For example, if you paid interest on a mortgage on a home that you purchased for your daughter in her name, this interest payment is not deductible.

- *charitable contributions,* to the extent that such contributions do not exceed 50% of your adjusted gross income, and subject to some further limitations based on the type of organization to which the contribution was made and the type of property donated.
- *casualty losses,* subject to a $100 floor for each loss and only to the extent that such losses exceed 10% of adjusted gross income. A loss from casualty arises from an event due to some sudden, unexpected, or unusual cause.
- *moving expenses* claimed by an employee or self-employed individual, provided the move is related to the commencement of work at a new location. To qualify for the moving expense deduction, you must meet a distance test, a length of employment test, and a commencement of work test.
- *impairment-related work expenses* of a handicapped individual. These include payments for attendant care services at the handicapped person's place of employment and other expenses that are necessary for the person to be able to work.

If you consider these deductions carefully, they are not likely to add up to the amount permitted for the standard deduction, which for a married person filing a joint return is $5,000—with the exception of the sizable deduction that homeowners will get for the interest paid on the home mortgage for the "principal residence" (which, as we have seen, can actually be your home AND a vacation home).

In the early years of a mortgage, most of the payment consists of interest. This means that much of the cost of living in your house (a cost which, if you were renting, would be nondeductible rent) can be deducted from your income tax. If you are purchasing a home and the mortgage is not in its last years, when the interest on the mortgage amounts to very little, it will almost certainly be to your advantage to itemize your deductions and reduce your income tax burden.

Obviously the higher your income, the greater percentage of tax you pay on that income, because of the "progressive" nature of our tax structure—certainly a strange definition of the word progressive if ever one existed. Thus the higher your tax bracket, the more your personal deductions are worth. For example, if you are in the 15% marginal bracket, $1 of deduction saves you only 15 cents. If, however, you are in the 28% marginal tax bracket, $1 of deduction saves you 28 cents.

When we say that the federal income tax is a progressive tax, we mean that the rate of taxation is higher on the last increment of taxable income than on previous increments. For example, Schedule Y of the Internal Revenue Code, the Tax Schedule for joint returns and surviving spouses, indicates that you will pay tax at the rate of 15% on the first $29,750 of your income if you file a joint return. On that portion of your income above $29,750 and below $71,900, you will pay taxes at the rate of 28%. If your income exceeds $29,750, that 15% tax for the first bracket has already been calculated for you ($4,462.50), and you are told you will pay 28% on your income that exceeds $29,750.

Therefore, if you are married and filing jointly with your spouse and your income, after all deductions and exclusions, is $35,000, your tax will be calculated as follows:

Tax on first $29,750 (from Schedule Y)	$4,462.50
Tax on all income over $29,750 ($35,000 − $29,750 = $5,250; $5,250 × .28 = $1,470)	$1,470.00
Total	$5,932.50

Note that while the tax rate on your last $5,250 of income was 28%, this does not represent your actual tax rate. You really paid slightly less than 17% tax on your $35,000 income. (And the $35,000 represents, remember, your *taxable* income, which is your income *after* deductions and exclusions. So you really paid much less than 17% on your *gross* income.)

Nonetheless, you are said to be in the 28% bracket because your last $5,250 was subject to tax at that rate. This is known as your *marginal rate* and indicates what the next few dollars (until you arrive at the next bracket) will cost you in income tax.

In calculating the effect of additional income or determining

145

what additional deductions may save you, use this marginal rate, because any additional money you would have or any money you will be deducting from your income will come from this last $5,250 of your income. Therefore, in the example we have just given, you are in the "28% marginal tax bracket," and every $1 of itemized deductions is worth 28 cents to you in tax savings.

To calculate the complete value to you of deductions and additional income, you must add the rate of state income tax you will be paying on your last increment of income to this marginal rate. When you have added these together to get a single rate, you will then know the exact cost of additional income or the exact value of additional deductions to you.

INCOME AND DEDUCTION TRANSFERS

To a limited extent, you can transfer income and deductions from year to year in order to make your overall tax burden as low as possible. Assume that your income has been running fairly steadily at $35,000 per year for the last five years. Then one year you sell some stock you have been holding for some time and have a taxable gain that will result in an extra $15,000 of taxable income, shooting your income up to $50,000.

The tax laws used to permit you to use what was known as *income averaging*, a method of calculation that allowed you to take a small tax break when you had a year of unusually high income following four years of substantially lower income. If you had one year in which your income took a jump of more than 20 percent, you could use income averaging. But the advantage to formal income averaging was limited. Nonetheless, it was (and still is) possible to do a little income averaging of your own.

For example, if you see in December of a particular year that this has been a fantastically successful year for you compared to previous years, you can try to bunch up some of your itemized deductions in this year and take them off this year's high income. As a practical matter, it is relatively easy to increase charitable contributions. You just write a check to charity. So if you are in the habit of making regular contributions to certain charities, you may want to make next year's contribution during the current calendar year. Thus the $50 a month you gave to your church for a total of $600 can be doubled by giving next year's $600 before

146

the end of this calendar year. Next year, of course, your charitable contributions will be down unless you choose to give again to your church or some other charity. But remember, we are assuming that this year's income will be significantly higher than next year's, so the deductions will be worth more to you now.

You can consider paying state and local income taxes in advance, because they are deductible from your income for federal income tax purposes in the year they are paid. If you have a child or grandchild who has a need for orthodontic care, go ahead and pay for the braces all this year instead of paying so much per month to the dentist. This will enable you to raise your medical expenses generally to the point where you can begin to take some deduction in that category during this year of high income.

Another deductible amount that can fairly easily be paid in advance is the January mortgage payment for the following year, which will include interest for December of this year, allowing you to deduct the interest from the year of higher income. It's important to understand, however, that it's necessary *actually* to make the purchases or payments that you deduct in the year of higher income. Simply writing a check and delivering it to your church after January 1 will not be sufficient, even though the check is dated before January 1.

Accelerating deductions is easier than postponing income, particularly if your income is mostly in the form of salary. However, if you have some outside business and it's possible to delay somewhat on collections, you may be able to push some income from one year to the next. The Internal Revenue Service watches extreme examples of pushing income, but if you have a small sideline business you've established because it helps you find business deductions for income tax purposes, the collections you delay making in December and hold off until January will probably not be so significant that the IRS will come down upon you.

DEVICES TO REDUCE TAXABLE INCOME

Income Splitting—How Less Becomes More

We've already discussed how the progressive income tax structure causes higher incomes to be taxed at a higher rate. The effect of the progressive rate structure is such that the tax on a $50,000 income is more than twice the tax on two $25,000 incomes. To be specific (and ignoring any difference in itemized deductions), a single individual with no dependents will pay income tax of $12,022 on a 1988 income of $50,000. Two single individuals with no dependents and with 1988 incomes of $25,000 will pay a total of $4,679.50 each, or $9,359 in income tax. Thus the individual with the $50,000 taxable income will pay $2,663 more income tax than will the two individuals each with $25,000 incomes. So the value of dividing a substantial income among several taxpayers becomes evident.

The simplest way to divide your income among a number of taxpayers is to make an outright gift of income-producing property. (You and your spouse can make annual gift-tax free gifts of up to $20,000 to each recipient. This "annual exclusion" is discussed in Chapter 12.) Assume that you are in the high income tax bracket of 33% and your child is in the lower bracket of 15%. You can give your child $20,000 worth of income-producing assets, and he or she will be taxed on the income at a rate that is much lower than your rate. (This only works if the child is not under the age of fourteen. Vastly simplified, the 1986 tax act provides that if a child is under the age of fourteen and his or her net unearned income exceeds $500, it is taxed at the parents' top marginal rate.)

Thus if you give your child, aged fourteen or above, $20,000 worth of assets that earn, say, $3,000 per year, your child will pay a tax of $450 on this income, whereas you would have paid $990 income tax on the same $3,000 income. Therefore the family's total tax burden (that is, you and your child viewed together as family unit) has been reduced by $540. As a bonus, you have prevented your estate from being increased by the $20,000 worth of income-producing assets and the continuing income from these assets over the years. So your estate tax will presumably be less when you die.

And, as we saw earlier, if the $20,000 of income-producing assets is likely to increase in value, that increase in value will not be in your estate but in the estate of your child. Suppose the $20,000 represents pasture land which is now being rented out but in just a few years will be city building lots worth $200,000. You have, by conveying to your child $20,000 worth of assets, kept $200,000 worth of assets out of your estate at death.

SOME TAX SAVINGS AVAILABLE TO SENIOR CITIZENS

You probably recall that for years a taxpayer sixty-five or older was allowed an additional personal exemption. The 1986 tax act changed this, and now a taxpayer sixty-five or older is permitted an additional standard deduction of $600. This $600 is simply added to the standard deduction to which the taxpayer is otherwise entitled. Thus, if a couple files jointly and both are sixty-five or older, they would claim a "standard" standard deduction of $5,000 in 1988 plus $1,200 (2 × $600) in "additional" standard deductions, for a total of $6,200.

Tax-Free Sale of Residence

Taxpayers at least fifty-five years of age who sell their principal residence may exclude from taxation up to $125,000 of gain realized from the sale of a residence. This is a once-in-a-lifetime exclusion, but it does permit a retiree to sell the principal residence and, instead of investing the money in a new home, invest it in income-earning assets and avoid paying tax on the gain. (Of course, any taxpayer, regardless of age, who sells his residence at a gain and reinvests the proceeds of the sale in a new home may postpone payment of the tax. But a taxpayer 55 or over may completely exclude—once—a gain of up to $125,000 on the sale of a personal residence.)

Annuity and Pension Income

The Internal Revenue Code specifically provides that amounts received as an annuity must be included in income. However, that portion of the annuity you have already paid for with after-tax dollars (i.e., dollars which represent income that has already been taxed) will not be taxed a second time. So you determine (with the help of the insurance company or your employer) how much you are expected to receive from the annuity, which depends upon your life expectancy and the annuity contract. Then divide the total expected return into the amount you paid for the annuity. The resulting percentage is known as the *exclusion ratio* and represents that portion of the annuity payment that will escape tax. The balance is taxable.

For example, suppose you are to receive an annuity which the insurance company calculates will pay you $15,000. (That is to say, the insurance company expects to pay $15,000.) You have paid $10,000 for this annuity. Each year, then, 66% ($10,000 divided by $15,000) of your annuity is a return of your investment and is excluded from taxation. The remaining one third is specifically included in gross income.

Lump-Sum Distributions from Retirement Plans

We saw back in Chapter 9 that proceeds of a pension or profit-sharing plan are subject to the federal estate tax upon the death of the participant in the plan if the proceeds are payable in a lump sum, unless the recipient elects irrevocably to forgo the exceedingly favorable income tax treatment ordinarily available for IRS qualified-plan distribution. This exceedingly favorable income tax treatment is the opportunity to use special "five-year forward averaging" rules, which amount to an opportunity to spread the gain over a period of five years. The rules for this five-year forward averaging are exceedingly complex, but suffice it to say that it can result in a significant tax saving to the recipient of the lump-sum distribution.

Another alternative available is to elect to "rollover," tax-free, all or part of the lump-sum distribution into an Individual Retirement Account. This gives the retiree an opportunity to invest all of the funds without paying any income tax and to watch them grow in an IRA until a later time, when the funds can be withdrawn and tax then paid.

This area is one in which retirees should exercise great care; they should never attempt to handle its complexities themselves. If ever a tax adviser is needed, it is for these decisions.

AUDITS OF FEDERAL INCOME TAX RETURNS

Because so many returns are filed by retirees and middle-income employees it is unlikely one of these returns will be subjected to an audit. However, because these returns can be audited in such a brief time, a larger percentage of middle-income persons' and retirees' returns are audited than might otherwise seem

Table 11-1

Average Itemized Deductions for 1985 by
Adjusted Gross Income Ranges

Adjusted Gross Income Ranges			Medical Expenses	Taxes	Contri-butions	Interest
Under $5,000			$ 3,165	640	438	3,425
$ 5,000 to	$	10,000	3,118	1,094	607	2,528
$ 10,000 to	$	15,000	2,393	1,259	787	2,757
$ 15,000 to	$	20,000	1,862	1,579	819	2,839
$ 20,000 to	$	25,000	1,713	1,830	809	3,220
$ 25,000 to	$	30,000	1,379	2,133	800	3,591
$ 30,000 to	$	40,000	1,639	2,696	891	4,121
$ 40,000 to	$	50,000	1,727	3,483	1,105	5,234
$ 50,000 to	$	75,000	2,799	4,750	1,575	6,730
$ 75,000 to	$	100,000	5,550	6,942	2,538	10,038
$ 100,000 to	$	200,000	8,500	11,034	4,237	14,419
$ 200,000 to	$	500,000	27,592	24,407	15,014	23,473
$ 500,000 to	$1,000,000		43,258	55,646	45,696	43,705
$1,000,000 or more			58,435	162,463	140,071	100,620

justified. Therefore, the threat of an audit is not one that should be ignored.

There are three types of audits. The *correspondence audit* is conducted entirely by mail and allows you to avoid the unpleasant experience of coming face to face with an IRS auditor and having to make on-the-spot reactions and decisions. The *office audit* is conducted at the local IRS office by an office auditor. The *field audit* is conducted at your home or office by an IRS agent. You have the advantage of being on your home turf instead of in the unfriendly surroundings of the IRS office. However, IRS agents are better trained than office auditors.

Selection of Returns for Audit

Income tax returns are "key-punched" (i.e., the information from the returns is placed in a form that can be fed into a computer) and checked for mathematical accuracy. The key-punch figures are later fed into a computer and compared against a rather complex set of standards. These standards include information from your past income tax returns, deductions claimed by

151

others in your income tax bracket, information sent to the IRS by others about you (such as the original of the W-2 form your employer sent to the IRS), and whatever the IRS's special areas of concern may be for this particular year.

The service has three years from the due date of your return to call you in for an examination. Thus for the return that was due on April 16, 1989, the service has until April 16, 1992, to contact you.

Average Itemized Deductions

Table 11-1 shows average itemized deductions for 1985, the most recent year for which figures are available, by adjusted gross income ranges.

If you have any deductions that are higher than the average deduction for your adjusted gross income range on this table, do not be overly concerned, but do be aware that this is a red flag which may cause the IRS to pull your return. However, if you can justify the figures you used for your deduction (as you certainly should be able to), then you have nothing to fear. Also, having deductions that are lower than any of the figures on the chart does not suggest that you should make up figures to fill in the blanks in future years. You should always be prepared to justify to an IRS auditor or agent the amounts you claim.

Pulling your return, if your itemized deductions are higher than normal or for any other reason, is merely part of the Internal Revenue Service's procedure for keeping taxpayers honest. Knowing we may have to face this sort of scrutiny helps us maintain a high level of accuracy in filing returns.

Also, you should be aware that a substantial decrease (a couple thousand dollars or more) in interest or dividend income without an indication that the income-producing asset has been sold or otherwise put to work may result in an audit. Other reasons for audits are a decrease in capital gain, a substantial increase in capital loss, increases in education and travel expenses, or moving expenses which are substantially above what you claimed in the past.

If you have a substantial decrease in income or an increase in any deductions or exemptions from a previous year, you should consider explaining the change in an accompanying document if the reason is not obvious from the other information accompanying your return. In most cases, however, any substantial changes from previous years will appear obvious from the return and accompanying papers.

If You Are Audited

If you receive a notice informing you that you are being audited, you should not panic. Spend some time reviewing your return and gathering all the verification possible for the items on it (which should be available in the same file where you put copies of your tax return for that year). If you are unable to find precise verification for some of your figures, again, don't panic, but obtain whatever secondary verification you can. If, for example, you are unable to locate the canceled check with which you contributed $500 to your church, you can use the church's records as secondary verification; the secretary or treasurer of your church can provide you with a statement showing that you did indeed make such a contribution.

If you are to have an office audit and it is inconvenient for you to go there, then by all means request a field audit. Remember, however, that the IRS field agent is likely to be much more competent than the office auditor. Also, you should be aware that inviting the agent into your home or office will allow the agent to assess you and your situation carefully and perhaps raise other issues. Also, if you are called for an office audit and the time is not convenient, you can arrange for an audit at a convenient time for you.

In dealing with an IRS auditor or agent, the best approach is to be firm but friendly. Do not volunteer any information, and be prepared to stand your ground, particularly when you have data or information that will verify your position. Remember that while you are being audited, you are entitled to bring up deductions you may have overlooked when you were filing the return. According to one study, about 5 percent of all audits result in refunds to the taxpayers caused by these overlooked deductions.

Remember, too, that under IRS rules, the taxpayer is not supposed to be audited on any issue on which he was audited and cleared during either of the two preceding years. The IRS agent or auditor will not be likely to have a copy of any previous audit, so it will be up to you to bring a previous audit to his attention and have the audit called off.

If someone else has prepared your return, you may want to have that person with you. If the person is a tax accountant or a lawyer, he or she will be able to represent you before the IRS. If, however, your return was prepared by a commercial preparation firm, a representative of that firm may accompany you to the audit but usually cannot argue your case for you. Abraham Lincoln once said, "Any lawyer who argues his own case has a fool for a lawyer." This is a pretty good rule in tax audits, and if you have any concern at all about your audit (and if you get an audit letter, you will have some concern), you should arrange to take some professional assistance with you.

If, after your audit is completed, you agree with the finding of the auditor or agent, you will be asked to sign an agreement form. This form waives your appeal rights and should only be signed if a small amount of money is involved. If you do agree and sign the form, however, you will receive a written copy of the audit report and a bill for the additional taxes plus interest within a couple of months. The IRS does not advertise the fact but it will accept installment payments if you can show that lump-sum payment would constitute a hardship for you. So do not hesitate to request installment payments.

If you disagree with the audit, you may request an immediate meeting with the auditor's or agent's supervisor and request that the supervisor revise the audit in your favor. If the supervisor does not agree with you, you will be notified by letter of your right to appeal within thirty days. If the amount of tax in controversy is $5,000 or less, you may take advantage of the new Small Claims division of the US Tax Court. The procedure for going to Small Tax Court is relatively simple. You merely file a petition requesting a hearing and pay a filing fee. You can obtain a free booklet outlining the procedures in Small Tax Court by writing to the clerk of the court, US Tax Court, 400 Second Street, N.W., Washington, DC 20217.

Even if you have no intention of appearing in court, it may be to your advantage to file a petition to take your case to Small Tax

Court. If the amount of money is small, the IRS may decide not to tie up one of its lawyers adjudicating your claim and may contact you to try to arrange a settlement. The majority of small tax cases are settled without going to trial, and the IRS often settles for about 50 percent of the amount it claimed was due in additional taxes. If you have a particularly good case, you may even be able to do better than this.

Again, the most important rule when facing an IRS audit is not to panic. You may, for example, be one of those unlucky persons whose return has simply been flagged at random to have every item on the return verified. This is a nightmare, but it is one of the ways the IRS goes about keeping us all honest on our returns. In any event, just because you have been audited is no indication that you have done something wrong or will end up having to pay anything. So stick to your guns, look the IRS representative squarely in the eye, and proceed to make your case.

It also helps to file your tax return at the last minute. Returns are selected for an audit on a first come, first served basis. Filing at the last minute with a great flood of other returns gives your return a better opportunity of being overlooked. Filing early puts your return into the office in time for additional scrutiny which may not be helpful to you.

PREPARING YOUR OWN TAX RETURN

Preparing individual income tax returns is not unduly complicated. (Although every time the IRS "simplifies" its returns, I find it adds at least another hour of work to the next year's preparation.) There is nothing quite like doing your own return to bring to your attention how high your tax burden actually is. With income taxes being deducted from our paychecks, it is easy to overlook what an enormous chunk of our pay actually goes to income tax payment. When you are required to deal with these figures at the end of the year in the preparation of your return, it gives you a better handle on what part of the tax burden of this country you are bearing.

Doing your own return also opens your eyes to ways in which your taxes may be reduced. If, for example, you noticed that the figures allowed in the sales-tax tables for itemized deductions appear to be somewhat low (or at least lower than you think the sales tax you spent in the preceding year was), then you may decide to keep all your receipts for a year and use the actual figure instead of the IRS's admittedly low estimate.

Even if you don't feel competent to prepare your final return, it may be to your advantage to work out a rough draft and take it to a professional for final preparation. You will gain the opportunity of reviewing the tax procedure and your own financial setup.

The income tax hits all of us in some degree or another. But with careful preparation and full understanding, you can reduce the impact of this blow. Remember—every tax dollar you save will be one more dollar for your retirement.

12

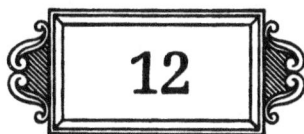

The Federal Gift Tax

The federal gift tax was devised to plug a loophole in the federal estate tax. Shortly after the estate tax law was enacted—in time to help pay for World War I—it became apparent that persons who were wealthy enough to be subject to the estate tax could avoid the tax by giving away their estate during their lifetime. If they died after giving their estate away, they would have no estate and the estate tax would not apply. So Congress moved quickly to create the federal gift tax, which taxed lifetime gifts at roughly 75 percent of the federal estate tax rates.

In the Tax Reform Act of 1976 (anytime Congress decides to increase our taxes, it calls it a *reform*—Congress must have its own dictionary), the gift tax and the estate tax were unified into one tax structure. And as you have probably guessed, the gift tax rates were raised to equal the estate tax rates rather than the estate tax rates being reduced to equal the gift tax rates. So the federal estate and gift taxes now make up a unified transfer-tax system which taxes the transfers of assets during an individual's lifetime by the gift tax and the transfer of assets upon death by the estate tax.

Since it would obviously be impossible to apply the gift tax to the myriad small gifts that family and loved ones present to each other on special occasions such as Christmas, Hannukah, birth-

157

days, anniversaries, and the like, Congress has provided what is known as the annual exclusion. This is an amount that may be given to each donee every year free of tax. The annual exclusion now stands at $10,000. This means that any gifts to any one person from any other person that do not exceed $10,000 in one year are not subject to the gift tax.

If the spouse of the donor joins in making the gift (if she signs the gift-tax return—she does not have to give any money), the amount of the annual exclusion is $20,000. So if a couple has three children and both the husband and wife join in making annual gifts to each of the children, they may give away $20,000 tax-free to each child per year, or a total of $60,000. This is a significant tax shelter, for it means in our example that in only ten years, a couple with three children can pass out of the estates and into the estates of their children $600,000 free of any transfer tax.

As we have seen earlier, the federal estate tax unified credit is equal to the exclusion of $600,000 from an individual's estate. Thus our parent with three children can leave an estate of $600,000, and there will be no tax due. The same exclusion applies to the federal gift tax. So the parent in our example could give away up to $600,000—in addition to the annual exclusion amounts—during his or her lifetime and not be subject to the federal gift-tax portion of the transfer tax.

But this "lifetime exclusion" is a unified exclusion, which means it applies to both the estate and gift taxes. So if you give away $600,000 of assets free of the gift tax during your lifetime, you will have used up your exclusion and there will be no exclusion left to apply to your estate tax. Put another way, if you give away $300,000 during your lifetime in addition to the annual exclusion amounts, and you die owning an estate of $500,000, you will have remaining only $300,000 of your lifetime exclusion from the transfer tax. In that case, $200,000 of your estate will be subject to the estate tax.

We saw in the discussion of lifetime gifts beginning on page 90 how a taxpayer in a high income tax bracket can transfer funds to a child in a lower income tax bracket and the earnings of those assets will thereafter be taxed in the lower bracket of the child. The difficulty is that if you give assets to your child in excess of the $10,000 annual exclusion ($20,000 exclusion if the spouse joins in the gift), you will be subject to the gift tax or you will have to

Gross Estate at Death		$500,000
Estate tax exclusion	$600,000	
Less gift tax exclusion used during life-time	300,000	
Unified estate-gift tax exclusion remaining	$300,000	300,000
Taxable Estate at Death		$200,000

use some of your lifetime exemption. However, by carefully giving away no more than your annual exclusion every year, you can pass significant sums of money to your child and pay no estate tax. The assets passed to the child will then earn money that will be taxed in the lower tax bracket of the child, and you will also save on income tax. In effect, you have given money away in order to save money.

Since the Economic Recovery Tax Act of 1981, the law provides that any assets you pass to your wife either upon your death or during your lifetime are free of the estate and gift tax. This is known as the marital deduction (see p. 135 for a full discussion of this deduction).

Even though the estate and gift tax rates have been integrated into one unified transfer-tax system (see pp. 121-123), it is still usually less expensive to make lifetime gifts and pay the federal gift tax than it is to die owning the property and have your estate pay the estate tax. This is because of a quirk in the law known as *grossing up*. Explained as simply as possible, the principle of grossing up works this way:

Assume that you have used your lifetime exemption of $600,000 and you make a lifetime gift of $100,000 and pay a gift tax of $23,800. The $23,000 used to pay the gift tax is not subject to taxation. So you have made a $100,000 gift at a cost of $123,800. If, however, you die owning $123,800 worth of assets, the entire $123,800 will be subject to the estate tax, since the estate tax is in effect a tax on a tax. You tax in this case will be $30,940, so that you will only be able to pass on $92,860 to your heirs because the entire $123,800 was subject to the estate tax. It has cost you $130,940 to make a deathtime gift of $92,860.

Obviously it takes a lot of money given away during your lifetime or in your estate to exceed the $600,000 transfer-tax lifetime exemption. Nonetheless, with real estate values what they are today and with the prospect of continued inflation, it is a matter that every retiree should be aware of.

WHAT IS A GIFT?

When they speak of a gift, most people think of the traditional giving of one small object to another without any payment being made therefor. However, to have a valid gift in the eyes of the IRS, you must have:

- a *subject matter* of the gift
- an *intent* on the part of the giver (known as the donor) to give the property away
- a willing *acceptance* of the gift by the recipient (known as the donee)
- *delivery* of the gift from the donor to the donee

If all these legal elements are present, you have a valid gift. If any are missing, there has been no gift. Of course, the intent to give can be presumed, as can the intent to receive the gift, and the delivery may be symbolic (that is to say that the delivery of a car from the donor to the donee may be symbolically accomplished by delivering the keys to the car from the donor to the donee).

Note, too, that you may have a gift that is intangible. For example, if you purchase a summer's worth of lawn mowings for someone else and the donee of the gift accepts your gift, you have a valid gift. (In this case, the delivery of the gift would consist of your telling the donee what you have done and his acceptance of your gift. So also if you cancel a debt owed you by the donee, this cancellation is a gift.)

So in addition to taking care not to exceed annual or lifetime exemptions, you must also be sure that you are aware of all the gifts you have made to a person. For example, if you give your daughter a $10,000 gift intending that no gift tax be paid because of the annual exclusion, and you have already provided her with membership in a health spa which you took in her name, then you have exceeded the $10,000 annual limit to the extent of the value of the membership in the health spa.

Before the 1981 tax act, any gifts made within three years of death were not considered lifetime gifts. They were considered gifts passing through the estate in order that the federal government might not allow you to take advantage of the grossing-up principle. Now, however, the tax law provides that lifetime gifts made anytime before death—even if it's only days or hours before—are considered lifetime gifts and the principle of grossing up will not apply.

The federal gift tax goes a long way toward plugging a loophole in the federal estate tax, but a small loophole still exists. You *can* avoid the federal estate tax by a program of careful giving. But, remember, only estates of over $600,000 (after 1986) need worry about either tax.

A WORD OF WARNING

As suggested earlier, it is best to keep most of your property until death. The average life span in this country is increasing with every census count, and many people live a long time after they have retired and after they have given away their property in expectation of imminent death. Often these people find that they not only have given away the property that brought them so much enjoyment but have also lost the solicitous attention of others that the property brought to them.

Therefore, in our discussion of a lifetime program of gifts and the advantage of giving property away versus dying owning it, we are assuming you have sufficient assets so that you will not miss those you give away. You should never give away property during your lifetime that you may conceivably need at a later time. Remember the warning in an earlier chapter on taxes: Never do what you don't want to do simply because it saves taxes.

13

Tax Shelters

In a sense, the term "tax shelter" defines itself. A tax shelter is any means of shielding (or sheltering) money or assets from taxation. (Although most books on tax shelters deal solely with income tax, it is also possible, as demonstrated earlier, to shelter estate assets from the estate tax and to shelter gifts from the gift tax.)

If, for example, income that would normally be subject to taxation as ordinary income can somehow qualify for taxation as a capital gain, this income has been sheltered from some of the income tax, since capital gains are taxed at a lower rate than ordinary income. Or if income need not be reported and therefore taxed when it is earned but can be accumulated until a later date and taxed then, this income has been sheltered from some of the income tax. This deferral device shelters money in two ways: (1) Income can be set aside during high-earning years when a taxpayer is incurring his or her highest tax rate, to be reported and taxed in, say, retirement years, when the taxpayer has less income and thus is in a lower income tax bracket; and (2) the money left untaxed can accumulate at a much greater rate than if the income tax had been taken out initially.

In both these examples, some income tax is paid, but in both instances the tax is lower than it might otherwise have been. Thus we say that some of the income has been sheltered from income tax. It is possible in some cases to shield all of certain income from income tax and also to come up with sufficient excess deductions to reduce tax on other income. That is the taxpayer's version of heaven!

The basic concept behind all income tax shelters is simple: Congress, in using the tax laws to accomplish certain nontax purposes, creates tax advantages for certain types of income in order to draw investors to those areas. For example, to encourage the sale of Series EE Savings Bonds, Congress permits the reporting of interest on these bonds to be postponed until the bonds are cashed. This attracts investors who want the advantage of earning interest during their high-income years and having it taxed when they cash their bonds during low-income years. Likewise, to encourage oil exploration and discovery, Congress permits the income from oil strikes to be offset by deductions for drilling expenses in dry holes. The resulting income from oil strikes is, then, largely sheltered from the income tax.

TWO WAYS TO SHELTER INCOME

Congress has formally identified two means of sheltering income from taxation: (1) deferral and (2) leverage.

1. *Deferral* has already been discussed in the example of Series EE Bonds. The idea is to defer reporting income during high-tax years until a period of lower taxation, such as retirement. Another form of deferral is the tax shelter that produces large deductions in the early years and little income. This excess of deductions over income is used to offset the taxpayer's other high-bracket income. Typically the taxpayer will "roll over" his investment into another tax shelter when the first tax shelter begins to produce substantial income.

2. *Leverage* is the use of borrowed money to control an asset many times the size of the investor's out-of-pocket investment. For example, if you buy a building worth $100,000 using $10,000 of your own money and $90,000 of borrowed money, you have used leverage. If the value of the building rises by only 10% (to $110,000), you have a gain of $10,000, or 100% of your actual out-of-pocket investment. (The IRS calls the $10,000 you have invested the amount you have at risk.) Leverage in tax shelters is important because it enables you to deduct all the costs of the entire asset and not merely the amount represented by your at-risk invest-

ment. (In this example, you can deduct the expenses of the entire $100,000 building and not merely the 10% of the expenses represented by the $10,000 you have at risk.)

In another example, let's say that you purchase a $300,000 building with a down payment of $5,000 and assume a mortgage for the remainder. If in the first year the business expenses of the entire $300,000 venture (depreciation, real estate taxes, interest, and the like) amount to $10,000, you could deduct this $10,000 from your taxable income. If your taxable income from all sources was $50,000, you could reduce that figure to $40,000 and the money saved by paying tax on only $40,000 instead of on $50,000 is $5,410—more than the amount of your at-risk investment.

However, the IRS will not allow you to deduct more than the amount you have at risk, so you can deduct only $5,000. But you have acquired an investment paid for entirely by Uncle Sam, because if you had not invested $5,000 in this building, you would have paid $5,000 in additional income tax. Thus you "shelter" $5,000 from the income tax by making this investment. (If your taxable income was less than $50,000, your savings also would be less, but you would still be able to shelter some part of your income from the income tax.)

DEPRECIATION

One of the problems with tax shelters that shelter more than merely the income from the tax-shelter device itself is that they are often damnably complicated.

For example, you may be using leveraging to purchase a piece of real estate. You decide you want the advantage of tax deferral in order to shelter more income than merely that which is earned by the building you now own. To do this, you resort to expenditures that are really only "paper" expenditures but that are recognized by the IRS. One example is *depreciation*, a deduction that is recognized by the IRS but that requires no output of money on your part. The theory is that the property is declining ("depreciating") in value by so much per year and that you should be able to deduct this decline in value from your income from the property. In fact, of course, most real estate in recent years has increased in value each year. But, no matter—depreciation is still allowed. Depreciation, then, is a paper expense which results in larger deductions than would otherwise be possible.

And suppose that instead of investing in real estate, you invested in some sort of equipment which has a shorter useful life than real estate. You would be able to take an even greater depreciation deduction each year. The reasoning is that the shorter the useful life of your property is, the larger the annual depreciation deduction should be. For example, if you have a $50,000 asset with a ten-year useful life, you are permitted a $5,000 deduction for depreciation each year for ten years. If, on the other hand, you have a $50,000 asset with a five-year useful life, you can take a $10,000 deduction for depreciation each year for five years.

LIMITED PARTNERSHIPS

So we come to what is known as the *limited partnership*, a business in which there are two types of partners: general and limited. The *general partners* are involved in the management of the partnership and are fully responsible personally for the partnership's liabilities or losses. *Limited partners*, on the other hand, are simply investors and are responsible only to the limit of their investment, very much like shareholders in a corporation.

The reason partnerships are formed to deal in tax shelters rather than using corporations is that a corporation is a separate taxpayer. If a corporation were to invest in a tax shelter, the corporation would first have to pay income tax on its investment income and then the shareholders in the corporation would have to pay tax again when the corporation's income was distributed. But a partnership, while it is a legally recognized organization, has no separate tax standing. Any income earned by the partnership passes straight on through to the partners and is taxed to them as individual taxpayers. The partnership itself pays no income tax.

So limited partnerships now exist for all sorts of tax-shelter opportunities. The general partners put together a fancy prospectus showing their investments and then seek limited partners (investors). As an investor, you don't need to know much about equipment leasing or real estate leveraging or indeed anything at all about the type of business the partnership is going into. You only need to know if you have the necessary money and if this is a real investment or a scam.

165

Reviewing a Tax-Shelter Prospectus

The document that offers investors an opportunity to become limited partners in the investment is known as a prospectus. Knowing how to read a prospectus can be extremely important. Are you getting into a valid tax shelter or one that merely is seeking to take your money and run? You need to know, then, at the very minimum, certain specific things about the offering being made to you in the tax shelter prospectus.

1. You should be provided with the names, addresses, and phone numbers of the general partners. If the prospectus is for a public offering (i.e., made to the public at large), the financial statements of the general partners must be set out in it. If, however, it is a private offering, the financial statement may not appear. In this case, you should ask the general partners directly for income statement, balance sheet, and what is known as a *sources and use of funds statement*. From these documents, you can determine the financial condition of the general partners. If there is evidence of financial difficulty, you will be alerted to the possibility that they may use partnership funds to satisfy some of their own obligations.

2. You will also want to check out the general partners' track record in past partnerships. The prospectus of a public offering will generally set out this information in sufficient detail. If the partnership is a private offering, you will have to ask directly for detailed information. Do not be satisfied until you have the information you need.

3. Once you have satisfied yourself with regard to the information provided by the general partners themselves, you will want to inquire of previous investors with the general partners. Ask them about their experience with the general partners, if they generally come through with promises; whether the partnership has been audited by the IRS, and if so with what results; and how cooperative the general partners are with requests for information, regular reports, and distribution checks. Ask also whether these previous investors are investing in the partnership you are checking out and if not, why not. Finally, ask the bottom line: Would they recommend that you invest with these general partners?

4. Look into the expertise of the general partners. If this is a real estate enterprise, have they been involved in real estate before? Do they know the turf or are they out on a wild-goose chase?

166

5. Check on the general partners' credit rating. Check out bank references, accounting references, and legal references.
6. Once you have assured yourself with regard to the general partners (and the previous questions are only a few of those you should ask—you need the advice of your lawyer, accountant, or other financial adviser), inquire into the offering itself. Determine the nature of the loans and any important loan terms. Note whether there are any loans to or from the general partners.
7. Review the partnership agreement and be sure of your rights as a limited partner, including the right to resell your interest or redeem it.
8. Inquire into the controls the limited partners have over the general partners and the business itself, such as the right to elect or to remove the general partners or terminate the partnership.
9. Note especially whether the partnership agreement limits the general partners' liability.
10. Find out what type of reports must be made by the general partners and the frequency of the reports.

In short, go into a limited partnership full of questions and with your eyes wide open. After you and your counsel have made a thorough examination and raised all the questions and answered them to your satisfaction, seek the opinions of others who are involved in the same field of endeavor. Ask them for their estimate of the risk involved. Get a pretty fair idea of the tax write-offs and annual cash flow you can expect.

Be warned! Tax shelters are extremely complicated, touchy, and risky. Never get involved in a tax-shelter deal because someone telephones you and offers you an "insider's chance." Telephone solicitation by investment crooks is a constant problem. A recent popular scam has been the high-pressure "boiler-room" operation in which salesmen telephone and offer to help investors apply for oil- and gas-lease lotteries conducted by the Department of the Interior. This is a bad deal for two reasons: (1) You don't need any help to file for such leases; and (2) most of the leases available now are lapsed leases in areas that hold no potential for oil or gas development.

Another dubious deal often promoted by phone is deferred delivery contracts on commodities. The suggestion is that the investor is buying into a form of commodity *futures contract*, a binding contract to purchase the commodity. Actually the investor is buying a commodity *option,* a mere agreement to purchase the commodity at an agreed price on an agreed date. Agricultural commodity options have been illegal to trade in this country since the 1930s!

Metals options—another common fraudulent offering—cannot be sold legally in the United States except by a handful of recognized metals dealers. These dealers do no operate out of telephone "boiler rooms."

Another wrinkle on tax shelters is provided by promoters who sell Bibles, paintings, or lithographs to investors at what they claim to be wholesale prices. After the investor holds the asset for a year, he is supposed to donate it to a charitable organization and deduct the contribution on his tax return. The amount of the deduction is to be based on an inflated appraisal the promoter has provided and which is supposed to be based on the market value of the item. The fact is that in the absence of any open market for the painting or lithograph, the value of the asset is usually the purchase price, which results in no tax saving.

The lesson, then, should be plain: Beware of *any* tax-shelter investment! There are some good ones out there, but be careful.

HOW THE IRS LOOKS AT TAX SHELTERS

The IRS has declared war on "abusive" tax shelters—that is, tax shelters with no purpose but to create tax deductions. The idea is that tax savings should not be the only thing produced by a tax shelter. A valid tax shelter must be a scheme reasonably designed to produce a profit. And as a practical matter, if a tax-shelter investment loses money, you may find yourself losing more in the investment than you gain from the tax saving.

One reason for this situation is the "at risk" rule (see p. 165). This rule provides that you may not take any greater loss as a deduction than the amount of money you have invested or have "at risk." Thus if you have made a $3,000 investment in a tax shelter and have a paper loss of $7,000, you may only take $3,000 as a tax deduction in that year. The remaining $4,000 must be carried on to the next year under circumstances which make it highly unlikely you will ever use it all up. So the possibility of investing $5,000 in a tax shelter and deducting $20,000 in losses no longer exists.

This makes it even more imperative that the tax shelter be, in addition to a shelter, a good financial investment.

A FINAL WORD

Tax shelters are useful devices for legitimately reducing your income and encouraging you to invest in areas which, if you're fortunate, will prove profitable to you and which are in the national interest, such as restoration of historic properties, construction of low-income housing, and development of oil and gas sources. But you must be careful that yours is a legitimate shelter—that it is a good business investment and that you are dealing with people who are honest and aboveboard and know what they are doing. As with any other investment, a tax-shelter investment must be a sound business move. Otherwise it isn't worth the shelter that it probably won't provide.

Finally, as you invest in tax shelters and reduce your taxable income, you will fall from the top income bracket of 50 percent to lower income brackets. The lower your income bracket, the less a tax shelter is worth. Therefore, each tax shelter that you acquire is worth less to you than the one before it, because your income falls with each shelter into a lower bracket.

14

The Corporation—
A "Better Mousetrap"

Suppose you want to engage in a business venture which, although it offers great potential for profit, also carries with it substantial risk. You are willing to invest all your excess capital and give the venture all your time and effort. However, if the business should fail, you would rather not lose your home, the family car, and your personal savings account. Moreover, you'd like to invite others to invest in your venture and to afford your investors some reasonable return on their money.

Your venture is ideally suited for the business organization known as a corporation. A corporation is an "artificial person" that exists separate and apart from the person or persons who own it. This means that it is also a separate taxpayer, and therein lies one of its advantages.

Almost any lawful commercial venture imaginable can be incorporated. You can incorporate your candy store, the campground you run, your oil and gas business, and any of a myriad of other commercial ventures. Incorporation is controlled by the laws of the state in which you wish to incorporate. To incorporate, you apply for a charter with the appropriate state officer (usually the secretary of state). In your application for a charter, you set forth the purpose of your corporation and give its name, designate who the officers will be, identify the incorporating stockholders, tell where your headquarters will be in that state, and answer any other questions that might be asked of you. Then you pay your license fee, and your corporation becomes a living, breathing legal "person."

But why incorporate? What are the advantages?

NONTAX ADVANTAGES OF A CORPORATION

First, there is *limitation of liability*. Liability is governed by the laws of the various states, but generally speaking, a corporate shareholder's loss in the event the corporation fails or becomes involved in some unlawful action is limited to his investment in the corporation. Members of a partnership, for example, are all liable totally for the losses which accrue to the partnership. Thus if you operate a business as one of five partners and the partnership incurs a debt of $100,000, you are personally liable for that entire $100,000, as are the other four partners. And if the other four partners cannot pay, then your personal assets, such as your home and car, can be taken to help satisfy this $100,000 debt.

In a corporation, however, you are liable only for the loss of the money you have invested in the corporation. Thus if you have invested $10,000 in corporate stock and the business goes under with a $100,000 debt against it, you will lose your $10,000 investment but nothing more.

Moreover, in a partnership, if one partner should commit a wrongful act against a third person, such as to injure someone through negligence, you may be liable by law to reimburse the third party for this injury. However, if one of the shareholders of a corporation gets into legal trouble, this will not involve his fellow shareholders except possibly to the extent of their interest in the corporation. In a partnership, on the other hand, as just pointed out, every partner is liable personally for the legal acts of every other partner. Moreover, in a partnership, every partner can bind contractually all fellow partners of the firm. But in a corporation, as long as an officer acts properly within the bounds of authority granted by the board of directors, only the corporation will be liable on the contract. The individual shareholders are not themselves personally liable on the contract.

Another advantage of the corporation is that *management is centralized*. One of the problems with running a partnership is that every partner has an equal say in the management of the firm. The corporation, however, can be managed by a few shareholders (known as the board of directors), while the remaining shareholders can devote greater time to the work of the corporation or merely hold their shares as investment vehicles.

Enhancement of efficiency is another significant nontax advantage of a corporation. The corporate form has some built-in efficiencies. There are rather extensive record-keeping and reporting requirements connected with running a corporation. These records and reports can lead to the kind of self-analysis that a well-run business needs periodically. Moreover, the legal requirement for periodic meetings of shareholders (which should never be ignored or faked with phantom records of meetings that were never held) can be helpful in stimulating periodic reviews of the affairs of the corporation and can lead to significant improvements in efficiency.

TAX ADVANTAGES OF A CORPORATION

The big advantage of operating a corporation, however, is usually in the area of taxes. To understand why this is so, let's look at a typical small corporation. First, if you manage a business as a sole owner or partner, you are taxed on all your earned income "up front." If you have an income of $50,000 per year and you leave some of it in an office account to buy equipment later, you are still going to be taxed on the entire $50,000. The money remaining in the office account will be what is left over after the income tax is paid. And the partners' individual income tax rates run from 15 to 33 percent.

However, a corporation, being a separate entity—an "artificial person" created by state law—is the "person" who earns the money and pays the income tax, not the people who own shares in the corporation or manage the work of the corporation. The people who work for the corporation—even if they are major stockholders—are employees of the corporation; they receive a salary for their services and pay income tax on that income at the individual rates. But any money not paid out in salary to the workers of the corporation is taxed to the corporation, if it is taxed at all.

And the corporate income tax rate is somewhat lower than the individual rates for portions of the tax schedules. For 1988, for example, corporations pay federal income taxes at the rate of 15% on the first $50,000 of net income, 25% on the next $25,000, 34% on the next $25,000, and 34% plus 5% of the taxable income in excess of $100,000 or $11,750, whichever is less. This works out to an effective rate of 22.25% for the first $100,000 of corporate taxable income.

The 1988 individual rates, for married individuals filing jointly (which are the *lowest* of all rates), begin at 15% for the first $29,750, rise to 28% for the next $42,150, and go up to 33% for the next $99,190. Thus a married couple with a taxable income of $100,000 will pay a tax of $25,537.50 ($16,264.50 for the first $71,900 and $9,273 on the remaining $28,100). A corporation with a taxable income of $100,000 would pay a tax of $20,000 (15% of the first $50,000, which amounts to $7,500; plus 25% of the next $25,000, which comes to $6,250; and 34% on the remaining $25,000, which amounts to $8,500, for a total of $22,250.) The corporate tax savings, compared with individual taxes for a married couple filing jointly, amounts to $3,288. And the savings would be even greater for a single taxpayer who does not have the advantage of the income-splitting joint return rates.

And there are other advantages. Assume, for example, that you earn $100,000 before taxes in your business in 1988 and wish to retain some of the income—say $20,000—to use for possible expansion of your business. If you are not incorporated and you are married filing jointly, you will pay tax on the entire $100,000. The $20,000 that you leave behind for expansion purposes will be $20,000 left after you have paid income tax of $25,537.50 on $100,000.

However, if you are incorporated and your business has a gross income of $100,000, your corporation can pay you a salary of $80,000 and retain the $20,000 in the corporation as corporate income. The corporation will pay income tax on the $20,000 retained at the rate of 15%—after all deductions and exemptions, a tax of $3,000. Your personal tax on the $80,000 salary will be $18,937.50 after all deductions and exemptions, for a total tax bill to you and your corporation of $21,937.50. By using the corporation, you will save $3,600 ($25,537.50 income tax with no corporation, minus $21,937.50 total income tax using the corporation). You have gained in two ways: First, the corporate tax rate is slightly smaller, and, second, you have split the $100,000 income between two taxpayers, you and your spouse and your corporation.

Other Tax Advantages

The corporation has tax advantages in addition to these.

Group term life insurance. For example, a corporation may deduct from gross income the cost of premiums for group term life insurance on an employee's life. To the extent that the base amount of coverage does not exceed $50,000, these premium payments are not considered taxable income to the employee. So if it costs $250 a year to buy a $50,000 group term life insurance policy, that $250 is a deductible item to a corporation (i.e., it reduces the corporation's gross income for tax purposes), but it is not considered taxable income to the employee. Thus the corporation, through tax deductions, lets the government pay part of the cost of group term life insurance coverage for its employees. Moreover, as we shall see later, if the employee takes the proper precautions, the proceeds of the policy can be kept out of his gross estate for estate tax purposes when he dies. Finally, there is an important nontax advantage to group term life insurance. Often this type of insurance can be obtained without the necessity of proving good health, so that an otherwise uninsurable employee can obtain at least some life insurance protection this way.

Wage-continuation plan. Also, a corporation may adopt a plan that will continue to pay the wages of its ill or disabled employees. Normally such a plan is funded through a disability insurance policy. The cost of this plan is a tax-deductible item to the corporation but is not taxable income to the employee. However, there is one important consideration: If a corporate employee pays for his own disability insurance with his own "after-tax" dollars, the benefits paid under this disability insurance policy will not then be subject to federal income tax, but if the disability income policy has been purchased with tax-deductible dollars of the corporation, any income benefits later paid will be subject to the income tax. This leaves an employee with "Hobson's choice": A disabled worker will probably need all the income he can muster and would be further ahead to have it all free of the income tax. Thus, you can argue, the worker should provide for his own disability insurance with after-tax dollars. On the other hand, a disabled worker will no doubt be in a substantially lower income tax bracket and the savings may be worth more when taken against high income tax rates. This is one area in which the worker must decide for himself which is best.

Health and medical insurance and medical reimbursement plan. As with the disability-insurance protection plan, a corporation also can provide for health and medical insurance plus a medical reimbursement plan which would reimburse employees for any medical expense incurred by them or their families. Again, the cost of these plans is tax-deductible to the corporation and is not considered an item of income to the employee.

The corporation, then, has a number of significant tax and nontax advantages. But there are some disadvantages.

DISADVANTAGES OF CORPORATIONS

Higher taxes. When compared to the sole proprietorship or the partnership, Social Security, unemployment, and workers compensation taxes are higher for a corporation, although only slightly so.

Sham corporations. The Internal Revenue Service is always looking carefully at corporations to make certain that they are not sham corporations which are merely vehicles for avoiding taxation. This is not a serious problem if you have made certain that your corporation is a true corporation with a legitimate purpose. But you must be aware of the problem and do all that is necessary to make it legitimate and keep it that way.

The "human factor." Perhaps the greatest disadvantage of the corporation is the human factor. Some personalities are simply incompatible with the corporate form. Corporations require strict attention to detail. To be effective, they must be legal. And to be legal, all the forms must be carried out with precision. Taking advantage of the greater benefits of a corporate retirement plan, for example, requires a commitment to contribute to that plan. Some people simply are unable to do this.

175

Additional expense and bother. Finally, there is additional expense and bother involved in incorporating. Lawyers' fees to start up a small corporation and to operate it on a yearly basis can soon mount up. These fees and costs and all the bother involved must be weighed carefully against the advantages the corporation will provide.

THE PROFESSIONAL CORPORATION

Just as a businessperson may incorporate a business, so now in all fifty states certain professionals are permitted to incorporate. (The law varies from state to state. In some states, people in all or almost all professions are permitted to incorporate. In other states, the law is much more restrictive.) Professional corporations operate very much the same way commercial corporations operate, except that a professional person such as a doctor, lawyer, dentist, or the like may not limit his or her personal liability by using the corporate form. Thus if a doctor incorporates, he protects himself from the unlawful acts of others with whom he might practice. But he cannot hide behind the corporation if he himself or some employee under his direction commits malpractice. In that instance, the doctor is held to strict personal liability. Most professional corporation laws limit the ownership of stock in such corporations to members of that particular profession. Thus only dentists may normally be shareholders in a dental corporation, and so on.

With these two exceptions relating to limitation of liability and stock ownership, a professional corporation is much the same as a commercial corporation.

"DOUBLE" TAXATION

One of the great myths involving the corporation is that of double taxation—that earned income is taxed first to the corporation and then to the employees or stockholders. The myth simply does not hold up.

Assume, for example, that you have a corporation that earned $50,000 in gross income last year. None of that need be taxed to the corporation if it is paid out in salary or wages to the employees or in deductible expenses to the corporation. It is true that the law will not permit unreasonable salaries to be paid to corporate employees or officers in order to avoid the payment of tax on corporate income, but if corporate salaries accurately reflect the value of the employees' services to the corporation, there should be no problem.

It is also true that income that is retained by the corporation as corporate income and then distributed to stockholders in the form of dividends is subject to double taxation. It is first taxed at the corporate level as corporate income and then later taxed to the individual as individual income. As a practical matter, however, in a small family-controlled corporation, a large part of the income of the corporation is likely to be directly related to the services of the people performing the work for the corporation, and this income can legitimately be paid out in salaries to the employees.

The corporation, then, is not for everyone. But if you have a small business and feel you could benefit from the advantages set out here, it just might be a fine way to save a lot of money.

15

Putting Your Money to Work

We repeated earlier the well-known truth that acquiring a retirement nest egg is a matter of saving small amounts of money over a long period of time. The shorter the time, the larger the amounts that must be saved. Table 15-1 shows how an investment of $100 per month will grow at different rates of interest over a number of years.

To use this table, you determine, as we learned in Chapter 4, what your financial needs will be after retirement and what income you can expect at that time. The difference is the amount you need to fill in the gap. Then you calculate the number of working years you have left until you plan to retire and decide what interest rate you can expect to earn on your savings, and you can determine how much money you will need to save per month. For example, if you have twenty years left until retirement and you save $100 a month, at the end of twenty years you will have $24,000. You can bury the $24,000 in a can in your backyard, and at the end of the twenty-year period, you will still have $24,000. Of course, if we have anything near the present rate of inflation, your $24,000 will be worth substantially less at the end of twenty years than it would be now.

As you can see from Table 15-1, however, if you can earn 6% interest on your money and you keep reinvesting the interest

Table 15-1
Future Values of a Savings of $100 per Month

Years	Amount invested	At 6%	At 10%	At 12%	At 15%
5	6,000	6,984	7,723	8,119	8,748
10	12,000	16,331	20,161	22,427	26,344
15	18,000	28,839	40,192	47,643	61,736
20	24,000	45,577	72,453	92,083	132,921
25	30,000	67,977	124,409	170,401	276,099
30	36,000	97,953	208,085	308,423	564,082
40	48,000	191,750	559,880	980,343	2,308,370

Example: Saving $100 per month every month for 20 years at 10% interest will be worth $72,453 at the end of the 20 years.

Note: Interest rates are compounded annually.

earned, at the end of twenty years your $24,000 will have grown to $45,577. And if you can earn 12% interest your $24,000 will grow to $92,083.

The question, then, becomes one of how to earn the maximum return on your money.

SECURITY VERSUS HIGH RETURN

All investing (or perhaps we should say all sane investing) involves a balancing act between high return on risky ventures and low return on absolutely safe investments.

The ideal investment, of course, is one with absolutely no risk and a guaranteed high return. But this ideal is never achieved. So you face the question of how much risk you can afford; then you can find out how much return you can get on your money with the degree of risk you are willing to accept.

Of course, you are planning for your retirement nest egg. And you can't afford *any* risk, you say. Well, there is risk and there is risk.

GOVERNMENT OBLIGATIONS AND BANK ACCOUNTS

When we think of maximum safety in investing our money, we normally think of banks and the United States government. Banks and other savings institutions (such as savings and loan associations) offer what are known as passbook savings accounts, which pay a low interest rate (in recent years around 5%–6%) and permit deposits and withdrawals at your discretion. Your money, up to $100,000, is insured by the Federal Deposit Insurance Corporation. (The FDIC insures deposits in national and member state banks. Not all state banks need belong to the FDIC, but if you are looking for maximum safety, you will want to make certain that your bank is a member of the FDIC. Note, too, that deposits in savings and loan institutions are protected by the Federal Savings and Loan Insurance Corporation or FSLIC.)

Another investment that has maximum safety is a certificate of deposit (known as a CD) issued by a bank or savings and loan association to mature in anywhere from thirty days to eight years. Interest is paid on the investment from the day of deposit to the maturity date, with rates generally higher on CDs than on passbook savings accounts. CD rates are based on the going interest at the time of issue of the CD.

The disadvantage of certificates of deposit is that you must tie up your money for a long period of time. If you withdraw your money before the date of maturity (and such withdrawal is not at your option but must be approved by the issuing bank), you lose a considerable amount of interest as a penalty. In a time of continuing inflation, certificates of deposit could lock you into an interest rate that is soon overtaken by soaring inflation figures. However, you still earn a higher rate of interest on your money with a CD than with a passbook savings account.

Another extremely safe investment is government bonds and other obligations guaranteed by the United States government. Of these, the Series E savings bond is probably the most widely known. These bonds, which are no longer available, were purchased on a discount basis. That is to say, you bought a $25 bond for $18.75 and on maturity received $25. (This is known as purchasing at a discount and redeeming at par.) You were required to hold these bonds for a minimum of two months from the date of issue, after which they could be redeemed at a discount anytime before the maturity date.

Series H bonds were ten-year government income bonds available in minimum amounts of $500. The difference between the Series E and Series H bond was that with the Series H bond, you purchased the bond at its face value and then were paid interest semiannually. Series E bonds were purchased at discount and no income was paid until the maturity date, when you received the face value of the bond. Then the difference between what you paid for the bond and its face value was your income. Interest on the Series E bond was not taxable until the bond was cashed. Interest on Series H bonds was taxable when paid.

The government now is pushing (and "pushing" is the correct verb) Series EE and Series HH government savings bonds as substitutes for Series E and H bonds. Series EE bonds differ from the old Series E bonds mainly in that the new bonds are available in denominations beginning at $50 (the Series E bonds began at $25) and the interest rate is higher. Time till maturity is eight years. A $50 bond may be purchased for $25. As with the Series E bond, interest is not taxable until the bond is cashed. Series HH bonds differ from Series H bonds in that the interest rate on Series HH bonds is higher. This interest is still taxable when paid.

There are also obligations of the United States Treasury (which are guaranteed by the government), which pay higher interest rates. Treasury *bills*, for example, are available in minimum amounts of $1,000 and can be purchased from the Treasury Department, from a local member bank of the Federal Reserve System, or through a stockbroker. They are issued weekly on a discount basis, with the price determined by competitive bidding. At maturity (which is 91 days, 182 days, or a year), the face amount is payable. Treasury *notes* have a fixed maturity of one to seven years. Interest is payable semiannually at fixed rates. For investments of over seven years, Treasury *bonds* are available on the same basis as Treasury notes.

In addition, there are a number of obligations issued by federal agencies such as the Federal National Mortgage Association, but they are not government-guaranteed specifically. Still, they are of very high quality, since government agencies never go under because of bankruptcy.

All these investments in banks and federal government obligations are "safe" in the sense that you are absolutely assured that you will receive the rate of interest stated and that when the investments mature your money will be returned to you. However, the problem with this sort of safety is that it is not really very safe in times of inflation. If you are receiving a 5% return on your passbook savings account and the inflation rate is above 5% for the same period of time, you've actually lost money—to say nothing of the fact that your interest will be reduced further by income tax. Thus the much-vaunted safety of certain types of investment is at best a myth and at worst a fraud.

One of the factors to be aware of is the eroding effect of inflation on your money. Table 15-2 provides the necessary calculations to determine what amount of money will be necessary after years of inflation to equal certain amounts now.

For example, if you plan to retire in twelve years and expect inflation to average 10% a year for the next twelve years, Table 15-2 indicates that you multiply today's money by 3.14 to determine its inflated purchasing power. Thus if you have $40,000 in income and want to know what the equivalent income will be in

Table 15-2
Multiple of Present Income Which Would Have the Same
Buying Power at Retirement (at Various Rates of Inflation)

Years until retirement	5%	6%	7%	8%	9%	10%	12%	15%	17%	20%
1	1.05	1.06	1.07	1.08	1.09	1.10	1.12	1.15	1.17	1.20
2	1.10	1.12	1.14	1.17	1.19	1.21	1.25	1.32	1.37	1.44
3	1.16	1.19	1.23	1.26	1.30	1.33	1.40	1.52	1.60	1.73
4	1.22	1.26	1.31	1.36	1.41	1.46	1.57	1.75	1.87	2.07
5	1.28	1.34	1.40	1.47	1.54	1.61	1.76	2.01	2.19	2.49
6	1.34	1.42	1.50	1.59	1.68	1.77	1.97	2.31	2.57	2.99
7	1.41	1.50	1.61	1.71	1.83	1.95	2.21	2.66	3.00	3.58
8	1.48	1.59	1.72	1.85	1.99	2.14	2.48	3.06	3.51	4.30
9	1.55	1.69	1.84	2.00	2.17	2.36	2.77	3.52	4.11	5.16
10	1.63	1.79	1.97	2.16	2.37	2.59	3.11	4.05	4.81	6.19
11	1.71	1.90	2.10	2.33	2.58	2.85	3.48	4.65	5.62	7.43
12	1.80	2.01	2.25	2.52	2.81	3.14	3.90	5.35	6.58	8.92
13	1.89	2.13	2.41	2.72	3.07	3.45	4.36	6.15	7.70	10.70
14	1.98	2.26	2.58	2.94	3.34	3.80	4.89	7.08	9.01	12.84
15	2.08	2.40	2.76	3.17	3.64	4.18	5.47	8.14	10.54	15.41
16	2.18	2.54	2.95	3.43	3.97	4.59	6.13	9.36	12.33	18.49
17	2.29	2.69	3.16	3.70	4.33	5.05	6.87	10.76	14.43	22.19
18	2.41	2.85	3.38	4.00	4.72	5.56	7.69	12.38	16.88	26.62
19	2.53	3.03	3.62	4.32	5.14	6.12	8.61	14.23	19.75	31.95
20	2.65	3.21	3.87	4.66	5.60	6.73	9.65	16.37	23.11	38.34
21	2.79	3.40	4.14	5.03	6.11	7.40	10.80	18.82	27.03	46.01
22	2.93	3.60	4.43	5.44	6.66	8.14	12.10	21.64	31.63	55.21
23	3.07	3.82	4.74	5.87	7.26	8.95	13.55	24.89	37.01	66.25
24	3.23	4.05	5.07	6.34	7.91	9.85	15.18	28.63	43.30	79.50
25	3.39	4.29	5.43	6.85	8.62	10.83	17.00	32.92	50.66	95.40

twelve years, multiply 40,000 by 3.14. The result is $125,600. If you expect inflation to average 8% a year for twelve years, you multiply 40,000 by 2.52. In that case, $100,800 in inflated dollars will equal $40,000 today.

In order to avoid losing money because of a rate of inflation that is higher than the rate of return on your investment, you need to seek out investments that pay a higher return or that will appreciate (increase in value) along with the rate of inflation. So given the built-in loss in these "safe" investments, some of the "riskier" investments may not be so risky after all.

COMMON STOCKS

A share of stock is an interest in a corporation. If a corporation has 100 shares and you buy 1 share of stock, you own ⅟₁₀₀ of that corporation. Similarly, if a corporation such as American Telephone and Telegraph has over 650,000,000 shares of stock and you buy 1 share of stock, then you own ⅟₆₅₀,₀₀₀,₀₀₀ of that corporation. A common stock is neither a risky investment nor a safe one by definition. It depends entirely on the corporation itself. An investment today in a giant corporation such as American Telephone and Telegraph (I have no connection with this corporation and own not a single share in it) is a safe investment, while an investment in a gold mine sold by a man with a 1930s-gangster-style hat and a loud pinstripe suit who insists that your investment be made in small, unmarked bills is probably pretty risky.

The argument in favor of purchasing common stock is that rising profits will produce higher dividends and share values than if the investment were made in, say, a bond, which only returns a fixed amount. This is true as long as the economy expands and the individual company in which you have invested does well. However, in difficult economic times or in times of poor management for the corporation or hard times for the corporation's area of business, a particular common stock can be a bad investment.

Then there is the emotional aspect. The market price of a share of stock is supposedly affected by the performance of the corporation in the past and projections about its future. But often raw emotion takes over and investors will flock to a particular stock, artificially increasing its price, or sell their interest in it, artificially depressing its price, for reasons that have no basis in reality. Moreover, stock prices on the whole fluctuate frequently and at times violently. Even a company that is doing well and earning a good rate of return will do poorly in a drastically falling market.

Following the stock market scare of October 1987, there was a mass exodus from the market by the "little investor," which includes most of us. Since then the market has shilly-shallied around a bit but has begun what many believe is its inevitable climb back to its pre-October 1987 levels. (And, if you believe many prognosticators, it will eventually soar above those levels.)

Whether stocks represent a current "sound" investment depends on which "guru" you listen to. But investing in sound corporate stocks for the long run has been, historically, a good financial move. Despite some serious weaknesses, the economy of the United States remains the strongest in the world. An investment in sound stocks is, indirectly, an investment in the American economy.

One problem many perceive in investing in the stock market is that trading on the market is done by stockbrokers who are, at the most basic level, salespersons whose income depends on the number of "trades" they can generate. When a broker suggests a stock to purchase, the recommendation does not carry any guarantee that the stock will be a good investment.

A major factor in making a gain in the stock market is the ability to guess what will be the next hot industry (although we usually try to disguise the fact that we are guessing with all sorts of computer printouts and the like). Technology stocks, for example, went through a tremendous runup in 1980. Given the difficulties in the Middle East, energy stocks have been picked by many for a tremendous rise, but the recent downturn in international oil prices has led to a depressed state among such stocks.

The point of all this (which will be quite dated within a few months, anyway) is not to give you tips on the market but to suggest that investing in the stock market is a complex business in which you should seek sound professional advice.

MUTUAL FUNDS

Assuming you haven't a great deal of money to invest in the stock market, and assuming that you are unwilling to take a risk by picking a company whose stock could decline in price just as steadily as you would hope it would increase, what do you do? The traditional answer is to diversify—that is, to spread your investment among a number of companies. This tends to reduce the overall risk, because one stock that drops may be more than offset by another stock that increases. However, if you have only small amounts of money, it is difficult to diversify. Hence the mutual fund.

A mutual fund is an institution through which your money is invested in the shares of hundreds of different corporations or government and institutional obligations. The fund is run by professional money managers who usually receive an annual fee of around one half of one percent of your total investment.

The big advantage of a mutual fund is that it offers the small investor not only the opportunity to diversify among many issues and to increase his opportunities of coming out ahead, but it also provides top professional management. The selection of investments for a mutual fund is made on a much more informed basis than that of any small investor.

There are all sorts of mutual funds, but they all represent the same sort of investment: They take money which is invested with them and invest it in other companies or in high-grade government and corporate obligations.

Stock Funds

So-called stock funds, which are investments in shares of stock in other companies, represent the opportunity to diversify your small investment among a great many more companies than you otherwise could. For example, if your mutual fund costs $50 a share and you buy ten shares, you have invested $500 in perhaps as many as a hundred corporations, something you could not have done with $500 otherwise. And you have a choice among stock funds. There are aggressive growth funds, which are looking for stocks with quick growth; long-term growth funds, which are looking for stocks with growth over the long term; and growth and income funds, which seek stocks that offer growth and pay income in the interim.

Bond Funds

Another type of mutual fund, which falls somewhere between stock funds and money-market funds, is the bond fund. Bond funds are invested largely in corporate and government bonds. Instead of investing in the stock of corporations, these funds lend money to corporations and the government and take their gain in the interest on those bonds. There are also more specific types of bond funds, such as municipal bond funds.

Money Market Funds

Money market funds have been the great performers of recent years, given high interest rates. ("Money market" is the name given to the large-scale borrowing done by the government and giant corporations for short periods of time.) By putting together large amounts of money to buy into the money market, money market funds are able to acquire higher interest rates than the small investor could acquire alone. The reason for this is that rates of interest on certificates of deposit and other instruments of debt on amounts over $100,000 are negotiable. Big money can always draw a slightly higher rate. So by buying with large amounts of money, money market funds make this rate available to smaller investors.

If interest rates begin to drop, money market funds will drop accordingly, and an investor in money market funds should begin to consider buying longer-term funds with the interest rate locked in or transferring investments to other sorts of funds.

Predicting Interest Rates

The difficulty of being able to forecast interest rates is overcome somewhat if you realize you needn't watch interest rates themselves. Rather, you should watch what big money market funds *think* the interest rate will be doing. In effect, what you are doing is allowing the money market fund's "brains" to predict interest rates for you. Many large newspapers carry a list of money market fund quotations collected by the National Association of Securities Dealers, Inc., which shows, among other things, the average maturity date of all the investments of a particular fund. Since money market fund investors would be likely to invest in funds with short maturity in a time of rising interest rates (in order that they might have their securities mature soon and be able to reinvest in higher-interest-bearing securities), and since the reverse is also true, the small investor can have some clue as to what is expected to happen with interest rates.

For example, if you watch a small number of money market funds in the daily listings and note that these funds generally appear to be lengthening the number of days of average maturity of their portfolios, then you have some indication that the managers of these funds believe interest rates are going to drop and are trying to tie up their investments in long-term securities to maintain the current interest rate.

Load Versus No-Load Funds

All mutual funds are sold in one of two ways. There are funds that have sales charges, and these are known as *load* funds. Then there are *no-load* funds, in which you must make your own arrangements for the purchase of the funds but which have no sales charge. Historically, no-load funds have done just as well as load funds, and since the sales charges or loads average about 8 percent of your investment, there appears to be little reason to invest in a load fund and pay the 8-percent sales charge.

CORPORATE BONDS

We have already talked about government bonds being a relatively safe investment. Corporate bonds represent another "guaranteed" type of investment. When you purchase a bond, you are in effect lending the corporation money in return for the corporation's promise to pay you a certain rate of interest and to redeem the bond at its stated value on the stated maturity date. Unlike a share of stock, however, a bond will not increase in value, regardless of how well the corporation does. (Municipal bonds are generally sold in minimums of $5,000 and corporate

187

bonds in minimums of $1,000, so diversification in bonds by a small investor is somewhat difficult unless you utilize a mutual fund specializing in bonds. Bond funds, like stock funds, offer a wide variety of choice in terms of how risky you wish to make your investment.)

In recent years, because of high interest rates and the slowing of the rate of inflation, bonds have done better than at any time in the past fifty years, but they are still not a good inflation-proof investment. One possible exception for those in higher tax brackets might be tax-exempt municipal bonds, which offer an interest rate that, although it is significantly below the going rate, is in reality much higher because of its tax-free status. See Appendix K for a comparison of the "real" return on tax-exempt investments compared with the apparent return on taxable investments.

REAL ESTATE

One of the "golden opportunities of the past two decades, real estate is not now considered to be a good investment except for those in the 50% bracket. The reason is, of course, that mortgage interest rates have marched back and forth between 15% and 20% with increasing regularity and the rate of inflation has slowed down, reducing the annual increase in property values which meant so much gain in real estate in the past.

Real estate has traditionally been one of the ways a small investor could get into an investment program and make some big money, principally through leverage and a bit of hard work. The purchase of a second home, a duplex, or a small apartment building to rent, provided you do all the maintenance, upkeep, and management, may still not be a bad idea as long as you do not have to borrow excessive amounts of money at today's rates, which will practically ruin any opportunity for coming out ahead on the investment.

It used to be that you could buy a duplex for $70,000 and count on at least a 10 percent annual rise in value. If you could get a mortgage for 75 percent of the house (in this case, $52,500) and if the mortgage was at a fairly reasonable interest rate, income from one-half of the property would mainly be offset by the deduction for depreciation and other expenses, and the rent would be sufficient to pay your monthly payments. In effect, then, you could buy a house for nothing. Now, however, with high interest rates, it just doesn't "cost out." The purchaser of real estate who is unable to put up much of his own money will generally find that he carries each month's payment at a loss, which is something that most small investors cannot afford. Moreover, putting up so much of your own money means you are losing the advantage of leverage.

If you have adequate cash to invest a substantial amount of money in a piece of real estate without having to borrow too much, you probably could do better with this money today by placing it in some other form of investment. So real estate, at least until interest rates come down, does not appear to be a very good investment.

PRECIOUS METALS

As the interest rate has gone up, the love affair with gold has cooled. Gold is an extremely volatile investment with a value that tends to rise or fall based on a great deal of emotion. In times of grave national emergency, the price of gold tends to rise rapidly. However, given the high yields available in the United States recently on much safer investments, gold has lost some of its gloss. One of the problems with holding gold or any similar investment is that, unlike corporate stock or money-market funds, gold does not earn any income.

While some investors believe that silver may be undervalued at present, the general attractiveness of other investments has made silver as well as gold a poor investment in the past. Gold and silver have some attraction for those who believe that the American economic system is about to collapse and that we will need something to use as barter in the days to come. Critics of this view believe you would be better off investing in canned goods and other means of survival if that is the real question.

DIAMONDS

Diamonds are the hardest substance known, but the price of diamonds has been anything but hard recently. While the value of diamonds soared in early 1980, they have since undergone a substantial decline in price, and this decline has been followed to a somewhat lesser extent by other precious gems. Investments in semiprecious stones such as garnets have had some following among speculators but have also suffered from the general decline in interest in gems.

COLLECTIBLES

The problem with investing in gems is that as interest rates have soared and inflation rates have slowed somewhat, there are simply better and safer ways to make money. The same is true of collectibles such as antiques, posters, paintings, and gold pieces collected not for the gold in them but for their numismatic value. The rule is that you should buy gems, antiques, or any collectibles only if you love them. If they appreciate in value and maintain their status as a good investment, fine. But if they do not, you at least have the satisfaction of owning something you have enjoyed possessing. Investments in collectibles and gems are not considered to be good investments now or for the foreseeable future. (This does not mean that you should not invest in things you enjoy but only that you should not make such purchases primarily for investment purposes.) And, incidentally, you may not invest an IRA in collectibles.

Part of the problem with such investments is that, being unique, they can be difficult to sell. This lack of liquidity is a serious drawback if you need money in a hurry, because it means that you may have to sell the collectible at considerably less than what you consider to be its top value.

COMMODITIES

Commodity trading is trading in agreements to buy or sell cattle, copper, pork bellies, Treasury bills, and the like at a future specified date. Most of the purchasing is done on the "margin," which is to say that you put up anywhere from 8 to 12 percent of the value of the contract and bet that the price will go up or down, depending on whether you are buying or selling.

In a nutshell, commodity trading is not for the inexperienced. For every investor who makes money trading in commodities, three lose money. This is hardly the type of investment that a person nearing retirement would want to make with what may be the only funds he has to set aside for retirement.

INVESTMENT RULES FOR RETIREMENT

Sound investing of funds for retirement is a matter of common sense. Some of the rules you should follow are listed here. You can undoubtedly come up with many more good ones.

1. Keep up to date on your investments. Review your holdings regularly in light of changes in the economy, the tax laws, and your personal goals and needs.
2. Be prepared to change your investment strategy in response to changing conditions. If you're stuck holding a long-term CD or other investment in a rising interest market, it may be to your advantage to cash it in and take a loss now in order to invest the money at a higher interest rate.
3. Diversify. Never put all your eggs in one basket. If you can't afford to buy many different kinds of investments, purchase a mutual fund.
4. Invest for safety; don't speculate with your retirement funds. But don't confuse a steady below-the-rate-of-inflation interest rate with safety.
5. Watch the direction the interest rates are moving.
6. Keep "time to maturity" of investments as short as possible in a rising interest market so as not to lose money as interest and inflation go up.
7. Lengthen "time to maturity" (or change the nature of your investments) as interest rates drop.
8. Invest as much as you can.
9. Reinvest as much of your investment income as you can. The multiplier effect is wonderful!
10. If you are in a low income tax bracket, don't bother with tax-exempt investments, which are only valuable to those in high brackets.
11. There is no such thing as a free lunch. You still have to pick your investments and keep track of them if you want to make maximum use of your money.

WHAT TO DO?

Whatever your plans are for retirement, the amount of money you have available is going to be one of the major factors in how successful your retirement will be. Perhaps only your physical health is of greater importance. Therefore, as important as it is to determine precisely what sort of investments are best for you, it is even more important to understand that you need *some kind* of investments. If you have assets that are not earning money for you at a faster rate than the present rate of inflation, then you are losing money—every day! If your financial situation is such that you can afford this loss, fine. If it is not, you need to make careful adjustments in your investment program and determine what is the best program for you. Since the creation of wealth is a factor of time and money, you can't afford to waste any time in beginning your retirement financial program. So put your money to work toward the day when it will permit you to quit working.

16

Life Insurance

Life insurance is a contract between you and a company under which you agree to pay a certain amount of money every year. In return, the insurance company promises to pay those dependent upon you a large amount of money upon your death.

Life insurance companies do not like to admit it, but in a sense, a life insurance policy is a bet. You are betting (albeit not *hoping*) that you will die before you have paid very much money to the life insurance company in premiums. The life insurance company, on the other hand, is betting that you will pay premiums for many years before you die. The company hopes that the premiums you pay, together with the income that is made on this money through investments, will be greater than the amount that will be paid to your family upon your death.

TYPES OF LIFE INSURANCE

The purpose of life insurance is to protect those who are dependent upon you from the economic consequences of your death before you have accumulated any estate, or from the loss of your estate by huge expenses at your death. Thus before you have acquired any large accumulation of assets and while you still have a family to educate, feed, clothe, and shelter, life insurance provides you with an instant estate in the event of your death. It also replaces that part of the estate you have accumulated that is eaten away by the expenses that accompany your death.

There are two types of life insurance policies sold in this country today, although they are called by dozens of different names and have untold numbers of special gimmicks and benefits offered by various life insurance companies. The two basic policies are *term* insurance and *whole life* insurance. (Whole life insurance is also commonly known as *ordinary* life and *straight* life as well as dozens of other less common terms.)

Term Insurance

Term insurance is "pure" insurance. It is a contract of protection under which the insurance company agrees to pay a certain amount of money to a certain person or institution if the insured should die while the policy is still in force. Term insurance is just like automobile insurance in the sense that it merely insures against a particular risk during the life of the policy. The risk in this case is your death while the policy is in force.

Since the likelihood of your death increases each year, the company's risk also increases. And as the risk increases, the premium increases. So in the typical term insurance policy, your premium will increase each year. The face amount of your insurance policy remains the same (i.e., the amount the company will pay in the event of your death), and the premium goes up. This type of term insurance policy is known as an *annual renewable* term policy.

The problem with such a policy is that the premium keeps increasing year by year, while your insurance needs may be decreasing. For example, your children may have graduated from college and gone out on their own, leaving you with less need for insurance coverage. In such a case, you may want to consider a type of term insurance known as *decreasing* term insurance. With this type of insurance, your premium remains the same regardless of the fact that your risk of death increases each year. However, the amount of insurance protection you have is decreased every year. Therefore, you will pay the same amount of money year after year for a decreasing amount of insurance protection as you grow older. The insurance company's risk of your death increases, and so the amount of payout is correspondingly reduced with each year.

194

Finally there is a type of insurance policy known as *level* term, in which the premiums remain stable for a period of time. For example, you may purchase a policy which provides that the premiums remain stable for five years, in which case you will pay for term insurance at a rate that is considerably higher than the pure term insurance rate for the first year or so of the policy. The rate for the policy in the last year or so will be considerably less than the pure term insurance rate. Overall, however, during the five-year period, you will pay the same amount in premiums that you would have paid for pure term insurance.

There are also other types of term insurance policies (about as many as the mind of man can devise), but these are the most common.

Whole Life Insurance

Whole life insurance is a combination of insurance and investment. The face amount of your life insurance policy (the amount of your "protection") remains fixed throughout the life of the policy. However, since the risk of your death increases each year, the amount of premium on a whole life insurance policy is much higher than the amount necessary to cover the actuarial risk of your death in the early days of the policy. Therefore, a reserve develops during this time.

In other words, during the early days of your whole life policy, a portion of each year's premium represents the actual cost of the insurance protection. The remainder of the premium builds up an investment fund known as *cash value.*

The cash value is invested by the insurance company and is used to pay off part of the face amount of the policy in the event of your untimely death. As each year's cash value increases, the amount of the premium which must be expended for "pure" insurance is reduced. The company is able to keep its premium level (i.e., does not have to increase the premium each year as your risk of death increases) because of the additional premium it has collected over the years and placed in the cash value.

There are a number of variations on the whole life insurance policy. *Limited payment* life insurance differs from whole life in that the premiums are not payable during the insured's entire life but for a limited period of time, after which they are said to be paid up. The way this works is that during the period when premiums are being paid, they are greater in amount than for a comparable whole life insurance policy. The company merely condenses the premiums necessary to provide the protection in a shorter period of time.

For example, you might buy a whole life policy with a semiannual premium of $250 at age thirty. Since it is whole life, you will pay this premium twice a year as long as the policy remains in force. But you could perhaps purchase a *20-pay* life policy for a semiannual premium of $400. After you have paid premiums for twenty years, the policy is said to be paid up and you owe no further premiums.

An *endowment* life insurance policy carries an even higher premium, and at the expiration of the premium-paying period, the cash value in the policy equals the face amount of the policy. When the policy matures, the face amount of the policy is paid to the insured.

PURCHASING LIFE INSURANCE

If you analyze it carefully, there are only two reasons to buy life insurance: (1) to create an instant estate in the event that you die before you have managed to accumulate an estate; and (2) to protect your estate from taxes and other expenses which may deplete it severely upon your death.

All other reasons commonly given for purchasing life insurance (to educate your children, to pay off your mortgage in the event of your death, to clothe your minor children in the event your wife is unable to work, and the many, many other reasons given by life insurance agents) are merely variations of these two reasons. If you haven't any estate, the purchase of life insurance will provide you with one upon your death. If you have an estate but fear it will be lost by meeting all the expenses which will occur at your death, life insurance will protect your estate.

Which to Buy—Term or Whole Life?

While some people suggest that you should never buy whole life insurance and at least one life insurance company recently announced it will no longer sell whole life during these inflationary times, it is not *automatically* true that term insurance is always your best buy.

Term insurance is pure protection at relatively low cost. It does all the things that whole life insurance will do in the insurance sense—that is, in terms of protection but not in terms of investment. So for a relatively small amount of money each year (albeit an amount that increases every year), term insurance gives you the instant estate you need or protects your existing estate from depletion at death. However, when you are in your fifties, the cost of term insurance approaches and passes the annual cost for whole life insurance of the same amount. Thus term insurance is not generally considered to be the most effective way to buy insurance you expect to keep for a long time. If, for example, you have acquired an estate and have no reason to expect that you will die soon, you expect to maintain your policy for estate-protection purposes until old age. In this case, term insurance may simply become too expensive to provide this sort of protection. (In purchasing life insurance, it is always a sound rule to purchase with the expectation that you will die tomorrow. Otherwise you may tend to purchase too little insurance. However, you must also consider the purpose for which you are purchasing the insurance. If it is for a reason that has more than a short-term purpose, you want to consider the possibility that you will not die tomorrow.)

Term insurance can be thought of, then, as temporary insurance to cover the risk of death while you are still young and while the insurance premiums are still relatively low and represent a small portion of your limited income. As you grow older and as the premium cost for term insurance rises to meet and exceed the cost of whole life insurance, you may want to think about whole life.

Participating Versus Nonparticipating Policies

Some insurance policies provide that if the company makes money from its underwriting activities (that is, from the sale of insurance and not necessarily from its investments), part of this profit will be paid back to the policyholders in the form of "dividends." These are not true dividends, however, but merely represent a refund on part of the premium paid. The Internal Revenue

Service does not consider them to be dividends and you are not required to pay income tax on them, but in figuring the cost of your life insurance, you will need to consider the effect of such dividends.

How Much Life Insurance Should You Buy?

One of the difficulties in purchasing life insurance is that it is such an emotional issue, and life insurance companies have, understandably, traded on this emotion. In life insurance sales pitches, we are given vivid images of starving children and widows who must take in wash to survive. But the purchase of life insurance need not be a matter of emotion. Determining how much life insurance protection you need involves a simple mathematical computation. It is not a pleasant one, for it must take into account the possibility of your premature death. But emotions to the contrary notwithstanding, it is still a simple mathematical computation. First you need to determine the total resources your family would have in the event of your death, including all savings, investments, life insurance, your wife's earning power, your Social Security benefit, and the like. Then you determine what would be necessary to provide for your family in the event of your death. This would include the cost of maintaining the family over the years, the cost of educating your children, and the cost of your funeral, burial, and last illness. The difference between your resources and your family's needs is the amount of life insurance you need.

If you are purchasing life insurance to protect your estate from depletion, you compute what the cost of taxes and other expenses would be at your death and subtract from that amount the liquid assets which will be available upon your death to meet these expenses. The difference, again, is what you need in the way of life insurance.

Appendix L contains a chart that shows the details on how to compute your insurance needs.

LIFE INSURANCE AND TAX PLANNING

Generally speaking, life insurance proceeds are includable in your estate for purposes of the federal estate tax. However, they can escape taxation in your estate if they are not payable to your estate (or for the benefit of your estate, such as to your creditors) and if you possess none of the *incidents of ownership* in the policy at the time of your death.

What all this means is that if you have completely divested yourself of any control over your life insurance policy during your lifetime and the policy is not payable to your estate or for the benefit of your estate, the proceeds will not be includable in your estate for federal estate tax purposes.

The term that is used to indicate your control over the policy is "incidents of ownership," a term which refers to your right or the right of your estate to any of the economic benefits from the policy. Incidents of ownership include:

- power to change the beneficiary
- power to surrender or cancel the policy
- power to assign the policy
- power to revoke an assignment of a policy
- power to pledge the policy for a loan
- power of the cash surrender value

So if you want to keep your life insurance proceeds out of your estate for federal estate tax purposes, you should take care to see that all these powers are owned by someone else, such as your spouse. And you must further provide that the life insurance beneficiary not be your estate or someone who could be said to "take for the benefit of your estate." An example of this might be if one of your major creditors was made the beneficiary of your estate or if your money was conveyed to a trust the purpose of which is to pay the estate tax on your estate.

Cross-Owned Insurance

Because of the rules just discussed regarding keeping life insurance out of your estate on death, married couples commonly provide that each be the owner of the life insurance policies on the other's life. For example, you convey all the incidents of ownership in your life insurance policies to your wife and make her the beneficiary of the policies. On your death, since you do not own any of the incidents of ownership and since your estate does not receive the benefits of the policy, nothing is includable in your estate. She might provide similarly for you with regard to her life insurance policy. Thus on the death of the first party to die, none of the life insurance owned by that person will be includable in his or her estate. However, when the second spouse dies, any of the benefits of the policy which have not been consumed during the lifetime of the second spouse or given away during that lifetime will be in the estate of the second spouse and subject to the estate tax.

Irrevocable Life Insurance Trust

If you and your wife both want to avoid having any of your life insurance proceeds taxed in either estate on the death of the first party to die *and* on the death of the second party to die, you might consider the use of the *irrevocable life insurance trust*. This is a trust to which you and your wife convey all the incidents of ownership in your policies and to which you make your policy benefits payable upon your death. Therefore, if you die first, the proceeds of your life insurance policies will be payable to the life insurance trust and none of the proceeds will be includable in your estate for estate tax purposes.

The trust can further provide that the income from the trust is to be paid to your wife during her lifetime, and she can even have some opportunity to use the principal of the trust. Then, upon her death, since she does not own the assets in the trust, none of the life insurance proceeds will be includable in her estate. The assets in this trust can be conveyed to anyone you choose when you establish the trust. For example, you can provide that the income from the proceeds of your policy be paid to your wife for her life, and on her death the trust is to terminate and the assets paid to your children, grandchildren, church—wherever you choose. So you will have skipped both your estate and your wife's estate insofar as the estate tax is concerned. Your wife can transfer her policies to the same or a similar trust and her life insurance policies will escape taxation in her estate as well as in yours.

The irrevocable life insurance trust is somewhat complicated. You need to have life insurance policies of considerable size even to be concerned with the federal estate tax, so you may end up with more protection against taxation than you actually need. Moreover, being irrevocable, the trust limits your flexibility. If your marriage comes unraveled later, you are left with the responsibility for paying for life insurance policies on which your estranged wife is the beneficiary and which you cannot change. However, assuming that your estate is large enough to be concerned with estate taxes and that your marriage is sound, the irrevocable life insurance trust offers considerable opportunity for tax savings.

Life Insurance Premiums and the Income Tax

One of the problems with purchasing life insurance is that the premiums are not deductible for income tax purposes. However, you can obtain some income tax deduction for at least a portion of your life insurance premiums through what is known as *minimum-deposit insurance*. With minimum-deposit insurance, you purchase your life insurance policy and, after some cash value has built up, borrow some of this money to pay for the life insurance premiums in whole or in part. You will, of course, be required to pay interest to the life insurance company on this loan against the policy, but the interest is a tax-deductible expense for income tax purposes. (It is only tax-deductible, however, if either the total interest on the loan doesn't exceed $100 or at least four of the first seven years' premiums have been paid in full without using policy loans.)

The minimum-deposit approach is only of value to persons in relatively high tax brackets, but it does offer an opportunity to take some deduction for whole life insurance premiums.

LIFE INSURANCE ON THE WIFE

A commonly asked question is whether it is necessary to insure the life of the wife if a young couple has small children and the wife is not employed outside the home. This is not a question that can be automatically answered yes or no; the answer depends on the overall financial picture of the family unit. The wife's ability to earn income is certainly a factor in the calculation of insurance needs. So, also, is the cost of child care while the wife is out earning income. If the spouse has economic value above and beyond her value as a housekeeper (and most wives today have), then most certainly her life should be insured. At the very least, also, there should be sufficient insurance to provide for the wife's burial and to afford some minimum care for the children during the period before they enter school.

I suggest purchasing more insurance on the husband than the wife, but this does not imply that a wife is less valuable. It is merely a reflection of the calculation to determine life insurance needs. If a couple can afford adequate life insurance on the wife, then by all means they should have it. If, however, they must limit their life insurance purchases, then they must do it in the direction where most of the money comes from, which in most instances will be the husband.

If both the husband and wife are working and they have no children and are not planning to have any, the need for life insurance is much less. Indeed, given both parties' money-making abilities, the absence of any significant debts, and the lack of any dependents to care for, there may be no need for life insurance at all.

Life insurance, again, is not an emotional matter; it is a matter of pure economics.

17

Putting It All Together

We've covered the whole subject of retirement, from the aging process through the emotional trauma of taxes, investments, and life insurance. What can we make of all this? What guidelines emerge?

TEN RULES FOR SUCCESSFUL RETIREMENT

1. *Careful planning is absolutely essential.* The sooner you start planning for retirement, the better. But it is never too late to organize your life and work toward established goals. Having a successful retirement without planning for it will simply be a matter of luck. Luck always helps, but planning can make luck come your way. If you're already retired, planning for tomorrow can bring the same positive results that pre-retirement planning brings. So plan, plan, plan ... the results will make you glad you did.

2. *Use the freedom of retirement to your advantage.* Every other aspect of retirement is secondary to the fact that you are now free to do what you want to do. All your planning and effort has been directed at giving you this freedom. So do *you* want. Plan where to live and how to live to suit yourself, not your children or grandchildren or anyone else. Make the investments you're comfortable with, not merely the ones that offer the best tax breaks or that conform to someone else's idea of a rounded investment program. Set your life patterns the way they suit

you. Remember, you only have one life to live. But if you live it right, one is enough!

3. *Know where to get professional advice . . . and follow it.* As we have seen, practically every area of retirement has complex problems which require the assistance of experts. Know where these experts can be found and how to get their advice. Then follow this advice—not blindly or irrationally, but within a conscious pattern that is consistent with your overall goals.

4. *Keep track of where you are and where you're going—physically, emotionally, and financially.* Watch your money. Keep an eye on your physical condition. Be aware at all times of what you can and cannot do. Some things can't be controlled, while others can. Knowing where your strengths and weaknesses lie is an important factor in a successful retirement.

5. *Keep yourself healthy.* Work at maintaining your physical and emotional health. There is abundant evidence that retirees can help themselves enormously if they're willing to make the effort. Wishing won't make you healthy, but wishing and working to fulfill your dreams can. Don't smoke, overeat, eat the wrong foods, or ignore what's going into your body. Exercise, get adequate rest, and watch your diet. Keep your mind stimulated. You're as smart as you ever were (maybe smarter). Read good books, listen to good music, take some adult education courses or enroll in a college class. Be sure you can look in the mirror and like what you see.

6. *Live for tomorrow, not yesterday.* As exciting as the past may have been, the future is even more so. The future is where you'll spend the rest of your life, so concentrate on it. As long as you're planning for tomorrow, you'll likely be here to enjoy it.

7. *Don't try to make it alone.* The evidence that retirees with family and friends are healthier and happier than persons utterly alone is overwhelming. Friends and family may move away or die, but you can always make new acquaintances. The process of getting to know new people can be one of the most stimulating experiences of retirement. With rare exceptions, there is no reason for anyone to be alone except by choice.

8. *Keep your sense of humor.* A good many things all of us do in the most serious vein are downright funny (to say nothing about silly). Learn to look for this humor and enjoy it. Be especially alert for the humor within yourself. No one likes a grump, but almost everyone loves someone with a sense of humor.

9. *Stay as independent as possible for as long as you can.* After a lifetime of calling your own shots, it is often devastating to be

placed under the authority of another. Keep your separate living quarters as long as you can. Manage your own money and make your own plans as long as you can. And when you must begin to rely on others, don't give up everything. Continue to participate in decisions. Keep control of your money! You may have to live with others and be cared for by them, but the fact that you have control of your own funds can give you a very real sense of independence. "Old" is not synonymous with "incompetent," and it may be up to you to make this point very clear. Remember, no matter how old you are or how much you may require the assistance of others, *it's still your life!*

10. *Make it easier for others.* There's never any excuse to be an SOB. If you have to rant and rave and rail to have people see things your way occasionally, do it. But don't make it part of your life-style. Life is often difficult for all of us, and if you can make it easier for those around you, do it. Kindness always comes back with interest.

Appendix A

Checklist for Apartment or Condominium

GENERAL CONSIDERATIONS

Accessibility:

Is it near
    a bus stop or other public transportation? _____
    shopping facilities? _____
    public recreation facilities? _____
    a public library? _____
    a college or adult education center? _____
Are there stairs at the main entrance? _____
Are there stairs in the lobby? _____
Is there an elevator? _____
    Is there an elevator operator? _____
    Is the elevator automatic? _____
    Is there an emergency stop control? _____
    Is there an emergency alarm? _____

Expense:

What is the
    monthly rent (apartment)? _____
    purchase price (condominium)? _____

monthly maintenance charge (co-op)? _____
Are there any other periodic charges (such as
    TV cable, maintenance, parking, etc.)? _____
Are parking spaces available? _____
    Fee or free? _____
Is there a laundry room? _____
    Are there sufficient washers and driers? _____
    Fee or free? _____

Appearance:

Is the neighborhood attractive? _____
Is crime a problem in the neighborhood? _____
Is the facility well kept? _____
When and where is trash picked up? _____
Where do residents place trash? _____
How often are hallways and stairways cleaned? _____
How often are windows washed outside? _____
Are there any signs of roaches or mice? _____

Security:

Are the approach and the lobby well lit? _____
Is there a resident superintendent? _____
    What are his hours? _____
    Can he be reached in an emergency? _____
Are deliveries made by separate entrance? _____
    Who controls this entrance? _____
Is there any security at the entrance? _____
    Are keys required to enter? _____
    Is there a buzzer-activated front-door system? _____
    Is there a doorman? _____
        What are the doorman's hours? _____

Fire:

Are there fire exits other than the main entrance? _____
Is there a fire alarm system? _____
    Is it connected to the fire station? _____
Is there a hallway sprinkler system? _____

Are smoke and fire detectors provided? _____
  Do they work? _____

YOUR SPECIFIC UNIT

Location:

Is it near the elevator, incinerator, or other
  source of noise? _____
Is it a long walk from the stairs or elevator? _____
Is it handy to the laundry room? _____
Is it handy to recreation facilities? _____
Must you climb stairs to enter the unit? _____

Security:

Does it have a door viewer? _____
Is the door steel or wood? _____
Do all outside doors have adequate locks? _____
If the unit is on street level, are the windows
  adequately secured? _____
Does the unit have adequate fire and
  smoke detectors? _____

Living space:

Are the rooms large enough for your furnishings? _____
Does the unit meet any special hobby, work, or
  leisure needs? _____
Does the arrangement allow for privacy in the event
  of company? _____
Is there adequate storage? _____
  In the unit itself? _____
  Elsewhere in the building? _____
    Fee or free? _____
    Secure? _____
Are there adequate cabinets
  In the kitchen? _____
  In the bathroom? _____

Utilities:

Are utilities included in rent or maintenance? _____

Are utilities on a separate meter for your unit? _____

Do all outlets work? (Test with small lamp.) _____

Is the fuse or breaker system adequate? _____

After the hot water has run for 5 minutes,
   is it still hot? _____

Is the bathroom ventilated? _____

Are any water taps dripping?

   Do sinks or tubs show signs of dripping?

Does the tub or shower have a grab bar? _____

Do all taps and commodes work? _____

Do all appliances work? _____

   Is there any rust beneath air conditioner? _____

   Does pilot light work on gas stove? _____

   Is ice solid in refrigerator? _____

Appearance:

Is the general appearance positive? _____

   Are any windows cracked? _____

   Are windows clean? _____

   Are shades and blinds clean and in
     good working order? _____

Is plaster clean and uncracked? _____

   Any evidence of water damage? _____

   Any evidence of recent patching? _____

Are paint and wallpaper clean? _____

   How often are walls repainted or repapered? _____

   At whose expense? _____

   Who selects paint or paper? _____

Are floors clean? _____

Recreational facilities:

Pool? _____

Sauna? _____

Tennis courts? _____

Racketball, squash, or handball courts? _____

Sunbathing area? _____

LEGAL CONSIDERATIONS (APARTMENT):

May you sublet? _____
  With permission? _____
  Without permission? _____
May you redecorate? _____
How are "damages" determined? _____
  Who pays for repair of damages? _____
Must landlord give notice before inspecting unit? _____
  How much notice? _____
How long is lease for? _____
Is rent set for entire period of lease? _____

LEGAL CONSIDERATIONS (CONDOMINIUM):

What are the real estate taxes? _____
How are taxes apportioned among unit owners? _____
Is there an owners' association? _____
How are officers elected? _____
Will the developer of unfinished condo guarantee
  the accuracy of projected expenses? _____
    Is there any experience factor to rely on
    for these expenses? _____
Are all owners legally liable for contracts made
  by the administrative board of the condo? _____
What about liability of individual owners for
  negligence? _____
Does any one person or organization own over 50%
  of the units (and thus maintain control over
  the condo)? _____
Must all unit buyers obtain their mortgages from a
  designated lender? _____

Appendix B

Special Housing Checklist for the Elderly

Does the building have stairs?   _____
   In the entranceway?   _____
   In the lobby?   _____
   In the unit itself?   _____
Are there steps within 2 feet of any doorway?   _____
Are stair risers no higher than 7 inches?   _____
Are ramps available to bypass stairs?   _____
   Do ramps have level platform at top of at least
      3 feet by 5 feet if door swings in?   _____
   Do ramps have level platform at top of at least
      5 feet by 5 feet if door swings out?   _____
   Do ramps have level platforms allowing for rest
      at least every 30 feet?   _____
   Do ramps have level platforms on all turns?   _____
   Do ramps have side rails?   _____
   Are ramp surfaces nonslip?   _____
Are doors at least 32 inches wide
   (to accommodate wheelchairs)?   _____
Do doors open easily, with a single effort?   _____
Is the approach to the building
   Level?   _____
   On a substantial grade?   _____

Are floor surfaces nonslip? ———

Is elevator accessible from wheelchair? ———

Are elevator controls accessible from
   wheelchair? ———

Are at least some of cabinets accessible from
   wheelchair?

   In the kitchen? ———

   In the bathroom? ———

Is the toilet accessible from wheelchair? ———

Are parking lots accessible? ———

Are parking spaces open on one side to permit
   room for persons in wheelchairs or on
   crutches or braces to enter and leave
   vehicles? ———

Do persons in wheelchairs or on crutches or
   braces have to pass behind parked cars? ———

Appendix C

The Gap Between Postretirement Income and Expenses

1 Item	2 Current yearly expenses	3 Estimated yearly expenses if retired today	4 Inflation factor[b]	5 Estimated yearly retirement expenses (column 3 × column 4)
Housing				
Mortgage				
Rent				
Taxes				
Insurance				
Upkeep				
Utilities				
Heat				
Lights				
Water				
Phone				
TV cable				
Upkeep on appliances				
Food				
Auto and transportation				
Clothing				
Health and medical				
Recreation				
Savings and investments				
Gifts and contributions				

Expenses[a]

Expenses[a]

1 Item	2 Current yearly expenses	3 Estimated yearly expenses if retired today	4 Inflation factor[b]	5 Estimated yearly retirement expenses (column 3 × column 4)
Income taxes				
Federal	_____	_____	____	_____
State	_____	_____	____	_____
Local	_____	_____	____	_____
Miscellaneous (Personal care, pets, etc.)	_____	_____	____	_____
Total Expenses				_____

Postretirement Income[a]

Pension benefits	_____
Social Security	_____
Investment income	_____
Other income	_____
Total Income	_____

Total Postretirement Expenses	$_____
Less Total Postretirement Income	_____
Gap that must be filled from additional source	$_____

a. If married, include figures for *both* spouses.
b. See Table 15-2 in Chapter 15.

Appendix D

Evaluating Your Pension Plan

1. Type of plan:
   ( ) Defined-benefit plan
       ( ) Integrated with Social Security
       ( ) Not integrated with Social Security
   ( ) Defined-contribution plan
       ( ) Integrated with Social Security
       ( ) Not integrated with Social Security

2. Contributions:
   ( ) Employer contributions only
   ( ) Employer and employee contributions
   ( ) Union dues and assessments
   My contribution is $____ per ( ) month.
                             ( ) week.
                             ( ) hour.
   My contribution is ____% of total contribution.

3. Participation required: Age: ____
                              Service: ____

4. Vesting:
   ( ) Cliff—full vesting after 10 years of service, with no vesting before then.
   ( ) Graded—25% vesting after 5 years of service, 5% for each additional year up to 10 years, plus an additional 10% for each year thereafter; 100% vested after 15 years of service.
   ( ) Rule-of-45—50% vesting for an employee with at least 5 years of service when his or her age and years of service add up to 45, plus 10% for each additional year up to 5 years.
   ( ) Other.
   ( ) I am fully vested.
   ( ) I have ____ years to be fully vested.
   ( ) I am partially vested (____%).
   ( ) I have ____ years to be partially vested.

217

5. Years of service calculated:
   ( ) ____ hours of work in 12-consecutive-month period
   ( ) Other (specify)
   The plan year (12-month period for which plan records are kept) ends
   on _____ of each year.
   As of _____, I have earned ____ years of service toward my pension.

6. Normal retirement:
   Minimum requirements:
   age: ____ service: ____
   I will qualify for full normal retirement benefits on _____.
   Benefit formula (how are your benefits calculated?):

7. Early retirement:
   Minimum requirements:
   age: ____ service: ____
   I will qualify for early retirement on _____.
   Benefit formula:

8. Late retirement:
   If I work beyond the normal retirement age, it ( ) will/ ( ) will not increase
   the pension that will be paid to me when I retire.
   Benefit formula:

9. Social Security:
   ( ) Social Security benefits are not deducted from my plan benefits.
   ( ) Social Security benefits will be deducted from my plan benefits to the
   extent of ____% of the Social Security benefit I will receive at retirement.

10. Disability retirement:
    Minimum requirements:
    age: ____ service: ____
    Benefit formula:

11. Survivors' benefits:
    ( ) Plan provides joint and survivor option or similar provision.
    ( ) Plan does not provide joint and survivor option or similar provision.
    I ( ) have/ ( ) have not rejected in writing the joint and survivor option.
    My survivor will receive $____ per month for life.
    If I elect the joint and survivor option, my pension benefit will be reduced
    to $____.

12. Death benefits:
    Before retirement:
    After retirement:

13. Applying for benefits:
    My employer ( ) will/( ) will not automatically submit my pension appli-
    cation for me.
    I must apply for my pension benefits ( ) in writing/( ) on a special form I
    get from _____ within ____ months ( ) before/( ) after retirement.
    My application for pension benefits should be sent to: _____
    _____.
    I must furnish the following documents when applying for my pension:

    If my application for benefits is denied, I may appeal in writing to
    _____ within ____ days.

Appendix E

State Requirements for a Valid Will

State	Minimum age	No. of witnesses	Holographic wills?	Does marriage revoke will?	Does divorce revoke will?
Alabama	18	2	No	No	Yes
Alaska	18	2	Yes	No	Yes
Arizona	18	2	Yes	No	Yes
Arkansas	18	2	Yes	No	Yes
California	18	2	Yes	Yes	Yes
Colorado	18	2	Yes	No	Yes
Connecticut	18	2	No	Yes	Yes
Delaware	18	2	No	No	Yes
District of Columbia	18	2	No	Yes[a]	Sometimes
Florida	18	2	No	No	Yes
Georgia	14	2	No	Yes	Yes
Hawaii	18	2	No	No	Yes
Idaho	18[b]	2	Yes	No	Yes
Illinois	18	2	No	No	Yes
Indiana	18[c]	2	No	No	Yes
Iowa	18[d]	2	No	No	Yes
Kansas	18	2	No	Yes	Yes
Kentucky	18	2	Yes	Yes	Yes
Louisiana	16	3	Yes	No	No
Maine	18	2	Yes	No	Yes
Maryland	18	2	Yes[e]	Yes[a]	Yes
Massachusetts	18	2	No	Yes	Yes
Michigan	18	2	Yes	No	Yes
Minnesota	18	2	No	No	Yes
Mississippi	18	2	Yes	No	No
Missouri	18	2	No	No	Yes
Montana	18	2	Yes	No	No
Nebraska	18	2	Yes	No	Yes

State	Age				
Nevada	18	2	Yes	Yes	No
New Hampshire	18a	3	No	Yesa	No
New Jersey	18	2	Yes	No	Yes
New Mexico	18	2	No	No	Yes
New York	18	2	Yese	No	Yesb
North Carolina	18	2	Yes	No	Yes
North Dakota	18	2	Yes	No	Yes
Ohio	18	2	No	No	Yes
Oklahoma	18	2	Yes	Yesa	Yes
Oregon	18	2	No	Yes	Yes
Pennsylvania	18	2	Yes	Nob	Yes
Rhode Island	18	2	Yese	Yes	No
South Carolina	18	3	No	Yes	Yes
South Dakota	18	2	Yes	Yes	No
Tennessee	18	2	Yes	Yesa	Yes
Texas	18b,c	2	Yes	No	Yes
Utah	18	2	Yes	No	Yes
Vermont	18	3	No	No	No
Virginia	18	2	Yes	No	Yes
Washington	18	2	No	Yes	Yes
West Virginia	18	2	Yes	Yes	Yes
Wisconsin	18	2	No	Yes	Yes
Wyoming	19	2	Yes	No	Yes

In many cases where it is noted that divorce revokes a will, it revokes it only as to the former spouse.

aOnly if a child is born or adopted during the marriage.

bAny emancipated minor may execute a will.

cAny person in the armed services or merchant marines may also execute a will, regardless of age.

dAny married minor may execute a will.

eSuch wills are recognized for service members on active duty and mariners at sea under certain conditions.

Appendix F

Devices for Avoiding Probate

	Advantages	Disadvantages
Joint tenancy	Simplicity and convenience. Affords sense of family unity when husband and wife hold assets in joint tenancy.	Reduces individual's legal control over assets. Limits opportunity to take advantage of tax laws without consent of joint tenant. Property can be dissipated by joint tenant.
Totten trust	Simplicity and convenience. Depositor has complete control over assets.	Applies only to bank accounts.
Disposition by contract	Creator has complete control over assets.	Generally limited to intangible assets (cash, insurance policy proceeds, etc.). Can be complicated.
Revocable living trust	Can avoid necessity of proving mental incapacity. Permits "preview" of estate executor's performance. Avoids necessity for appointment of guardian. Avoids will contest. Permits privacy.	Has no federal income tax or estate tax advantages. Can be expensive to create and operate.

Appendix G

State Individual Income Tax Rates

State	Range of Rates	Range of income brackets	
		Rate on first	Rate on excess over
Alabama	2% to 5%	$ 500	$ 3,000
Alaska	Personal income tax repealed		
Arizona	2% to 8%	1,000	6,000
Arkansas	1% to 6%	2,999	25,000
California	1% to 9.3%	2,000	15,500
Colorado	Flat 5% rate		
Connecticut	Capital gains tax only		
Delaware	3.2 to 7.7%	2,000	40,000
District of Columbia	6% to 9.5%	10,000	20,000
Florida	Corporate income tax only		
Georgia	1% to 6%	750	7,000
Hawaii	2.25% to 10%	1,500	20,500
Idaho	2% to 8.2%	1,000	20,000
Illinois	2.5% flat rate		
Indiana	3.4% flat rate		
Iowa	.004% to .0998%	1,000	45,000
Kansas	4.8% to 6.1%	27,500	27,500
Kentucky	2% to 6%	3,000	50,000
Louisiana	2% to 6%	10,000	50,000
Maine	Tax rate depends on filing status		
Maryland	2% to 5%	1,000	3,000
Massachusetts	Dividend & interest income—flat 10% rate		
	All other income—flat 5% rate		
Michigan	6.6% flat rate		
Minnesota	6% to 9%	19,000	19,000
Mississippi	3% to 5%	5,000	10,000

State	Range of Rates	Range of income brackets	
		Rate on first	Rate on excess over
Missouri	1.5% to 6%	1,000	9,000
Montana	2% to 11%	1,000	35,000
Nebraska	2% to 5%	Four-tier progressive schedule set annually by legislature	
Nevada		No state income tax	
New Hampshire		No state income tax	
New Jersey	2% to 3.5%	20,000	50,000
New Mexico	1.8% to 8.5%	4,000	32,000
New York	2% to 8.75%	1,000	14,000
North Carolina	3% to 7%	2,000	10,000
North Dakota	2.67% to 12%	3,000	50,000
Ohio	.743% to 6.9%	4,999	100,000
Oklahoma	.5% to 6%	1,000	7,500
Oregon	5% to 9%	2,000	5,000
Pennsylvania	2.5% flat rate		
Puerto Rico	9% to 43%	1,000	75,000
Rhode Island	21.21% of federal income tax liability		
South Carolina	3% to 7%	4,000	10,000
South Dakota		No state income tax	
Tennessee		No state income tax	
Texas		No state income tax	
Utah	2.6% to 7.35%	750	7,500
Vermont	25.8% of federal income tax liability		
Virginia	2% to 5.75%	3,000	15,000
Washington		No state income tax	
West Virginia	3% to 5%	5,000	30,000
Wisconsin	4.9% to 6.93%	7,500	15,000
Wyoming		No state income tax	

Appendix H

State Inheritance and Estate Taxes

State	Type of tax[a]	Surviving spouse exemption[b]	Surviving spouse rates[c]	Gift tax?[d]
Alabama	Credit estate tax			No
Alaska	Credit estate tax			No
Arizona	Credit estate tax			No
Arkansas	Credit estate tax			No
California	Credit estate tax			No
Colorado	Credit estate tax			No
Connecticut	Succession and transfer tax	300,000	5%–8%	No
	Credit estate tax			
Delaware	Inheritance	70,000	2%–4%	Yes
	Credit estate tax			
District of Columbia	Inheritance	5,000	1%–8%	No
	Credit estate tax			
Florida	Credit estate tax			No
Georgia	Credit extate tax			No
Hawaii	Inheritance		2%–7%	No
Idaho	Inheritance	50,000	2%–15%	No
	Credit estate tax			
Illinois	Credit estate tax			No
Indiana	Inheritance	All		No
Iowa	Inheritance	⅔ of tax due	1%–8%	No
	Credit estate tax			
Kansas	Inheritance	All		No
	Credit estate tax			

State	Type of tax[a]	Surviving spouse exemption[b]	Surviving spouse rates[c]	Gift tax?[d]
Kentucky	Inheritance	50,000		No
	Credit estate tax			
Louisiana	Inheritance	25,000	2%–3%	Yes
	Credit estate tax			
Maine	Inheritance	50,000	5%–10%	No
	Credit estate tax			
Maryland	Inheritance	150	1%	No
	Credit estate tax			
Massachusetts	Estate	Up to ½ adjusted gross estate		5%–15%
No	Credit estate tax			
Michigan	Inheritance	65,000	2%–10%	No
	Credit estate tax			
Minnesota	Credit estate tax			No
Mississippi	Estate	None	1%–16%	No
Missouri	Credit estate tax			No
Montana	Inheritance	All		No
Nebraska	Inheritance	All		No
	Credit estate tax			
Nevada	No state death tax			No
New Hampshire	Inheritance	All		No
	Credit estate tax			
New Jersey	Inheritance	15,000	2%–16%	No
	Credit estate tax			
New Mexico	Credit estate tax			No
New York	Estate	All		Yes
	Credit estate tax			
North Carolina	Inheritance	All		Yes
	Credit estate tax			
North Dakota	Credit estate tax			No
Ohio	Estate	60,000	2%–7%	No
	Credit estate tax			
Oklahoma	Estate	All		Yes
	Credit estate tax			
Oregon	Credit estate tax		12%	Yes
Pennsylvania	Inheritance	Property owned in joint tenancy with spouse	6%	No
	Credit estate tax			
Rhode Island	Estate	175,000	2%–9%	No
	Credit Estate tax			
South Carolina	Estate	All		Yes
	Credit estate tax			

State	Type of tax[a]	Surviving spouse exemption[b]	Surviving spouse rates[c]	Gift tax?[d]
South Dakota	Inheritance Credit estate tax	All		No
Tennessee	Inheritance Credit estate tax	600,000	5 ½%–9 ½%	Yes
Texas	Credit estate tax			No
Utah	Credit estate tax			No
Vermont	Credit estate tax			Yes
Virginia	Credit estate tax			No
Washington	Credit estate tax			No
West Virginia	Credit estate tax			No
Wisconsin	Inheritance Credit estate tax	All		Yes
Wyoming	Credit estate tax			No

[a]Where the type of tax listed is credit estate tax, the tax levied is equal to the maximum federal credit for state death taxes. Where both an inheritance and an estate tax are listed, the credit estate tax is payable only for any amount by which the state inheritance or estate tax is less than the maximum federal credit. For example, if the federal credit for an estate is $10,000 and the state inheritance tax is only $8,000, the credit estate tax is $2,000.

[b]The exemption listed is that of the surviving spouse. In some states, the surviving spouse has a separate exemption, and in others the spouse is lumped in with other beneficiaries.

[c]The rates listed are the minimum and the maximum rates for the estate passing to the surviving spouse after subtracting the spouse's exemption.

[d]Most state inheritance or estate taxes apply to any gift made within three years of death.

Appendix I

Federal Individual Income Tax Rates

1988 Schedule X: Single Individuals—No Dependents

| Taxable Income | | | | of the |
Over	But not over	Pay +	% on excess	amount over
$ 0 - $ 17,850		$ 0	15%	$ 0
17,850 - 43,150		2,677.50	28	17,850
43,150 - 100,480		9,761.50	33	43,150
100,480 -		28,680.40	28	100,480

Note: The 33% taxable income bracket in the schedule above reflects the phaseout of the 15% tax rate that begins at the $43,150 taxable income level and ends at $89,560 and the further phaseout of the taxpayer's one exemption beginning at the $89,560 taxable income level and ending at $100,480, at which point the 28% rate again applies. For each additional exemption (see the schedule below), the upper end of the 33% taxable income bracket is increased by $10,920 (as reflected in the $111,400 figure, below).

Phase-Out Ranges—Two Exemptions

$ 43,150 - 111,400		$ 9,761.50	33%	$ 43,150
111,400 -		32,284.00	28	111,400

1988 Schedule Y: Separate Returns, Married Persons

Taxable Income				of the
Over	But not over	Pay +	% on excess	amount over
$ 0 - $ 14,875		$ 0	15%	$ 0
14,875 - 35,950		2,231.25	28	14,875
35,950 - 124,220		8,132.25	33	35,950
124,220 -		37,261.35	28	124,220

Note: The 33% taxable income bracket in the schedule above reflects the phaseout of the 15% tax rate that begins at the $35,950 taxable income level and ends at $113,300 and the further phaseout of one exemption beginning at the $113,300 taxable income level and ending at $124,220, at which point the 28% rate again become effective. For each additional exemption (see the schedules below), the upper end of the 33% taxable income bracket is increased by $10,920 (as reflected in the $135,140 figure for two exemptions, and the $146,060 figure for three exemptions).

Phase-Out Ranges—Two Exemptions

$ 35,950 - 135,140	$ 8,132.25	33%	$ 35,950
135,140 -	40,864.95	28	135,140

Three Exemptions

35,950 - 146,060	8,132.25	33	35,950
146,060 -	44,468.65	28	146,060

1988 Schedule Y: Married Individuals, Joint Returns, and Surviving Spouses

Taxable Income		Pay +	% on excess	of the amount over
Over	But not over			
$ 0 -	$ 29,750	$ 0	15%	$ 0
29,750 -	71,900	4,462.50	28	29,750
71,900 -	171,090	16,264.50	33	71,900
171,090 -	....	48,997.20	28	171,090

Note: The 33% taxable income bracket in the schedule above reflects the phaseout of the 15% tax rate that begins at the $71,900 taxable income level and ends at $149,250 and the further phaseout of two exemptions beginning at the $149,250 taxable income level and ending at $171,090, at which point the 28% rate again becomes effective. For each additional exemption (see the schedules below), the upper end of the 33% taxable income bracket is increased by $10,920 (as reflected in the $182,010 figure for three exemptions, the $192,930 figure for four exemptions, the $203,850 figure for five exemptions, and the $214,770 figure for six exemptions).

Phase-Out Ranges—Three Exemptions

$ 71,900 -	182,010	$16,264.50	33%	$ 71,900
182,010 -	....	52,600.80	28	182,010

Four Exemptions

71,900 -	192,930	16,264.50	33	71,900
192,930 -	....	56,204.40	28	192,930

Five Exemptions

71,900 -	192,920	16,264.50	33	71,900
203,850 -	....	59,808.00	28	203,850

Six Exemptions

71,900 -	214,770	16,264.50	33	71,900
214,770 -	....	63,411.60	28	214,770

1988 Schedule Z: Heads of Household

| Taxable Income | | | | of the |
Over	But not over	Pay +	% on excess	amount over
$ 0 - $ 23,900		$ 0	15%	$ 0
23,900 - 61,650		3,585.00	28	23,900
61,650 - 145,630		14,155.00	33	61,650
145,630 -		41,868.40	28	145,630

Note: The 33% taxable income bracket in the schedule above reflects the phaseout of the 15% tax rate that begins at the $61,650 taxable income level and ends at $123,790 and the further phaseout of two exemptions beginning at the $123,790 taxable income level and ending at $145,630, at which point the 28% rate again becomes effective. For each additional exemption (see the schedules below), the upper end of the 33% taxable income bracket is increased by $10,920 (as reflected in the $156,550 figure for three exemptions, and the $167,470 figure for four exemptions).

Phase-Out Ranges—Three Exemptions

$ 61,650 - 156,550		$14,155.00	33%	$ 61,650
156,550 -		45,472.00	28	156,550

Four Exemptions

61,650 - 167,470		14,155.00	33	61,650
167,470 -		49,075.60	28	167,470

Appendix J

Federal Corporation Income Tax Rates

Taxable income over	Not over	Tax rate
$ 0	$50,000	15%
50,000	75,000	25
75,000	....	34
100,000		34 plus 5% of tax income in excess of $100,000 or $11,750, whichever is less

Appendix K

Computing Life Insurance Needs

Note: Asterisked items are optional; include only if appropriate.

I. Money Needed on Your Death
    1. Funeral expenses $_____
    2. Debts (excluding home mortgage and mortgages and liens on investments)   _____
    3. Estate tax
        3a. state $_____
        3b. federal   _____
    4. Add lines 3a and 3b   _____
    5. Cost of administration of estate   _____
    6. Aftertax contribution to family support   _____
    7. Years remaining before children reach 18   _____
    8. Multiply line 6 by line 7   _____
    9. College costs per child   _____
    10. Number of children   _____
    11. Multiply line 9 by line 10   _____
    *12. Semester cost of educating spouse   _____
    *13. Semesters remaining to obtain degree   _____
    *14. Multiply line 12 by line 13   _____
        14a. Total Money Needed on Your Death   _____

II. Family Resources Available
    1. Life insurance $_____
    2. Savings   _____
    3. Investments (less mortgages and liens)   _____
    4. Death benefit from employer   _____
    5. Number of years spouse would work during childrearing   _____

6. Spouse's yearly earning power   _____
7. Multiply line 5 by line 6   _____
*8. Profit from sale of second car   _____
*9. Profit from sale of home and move into smaller
    home   _____
*10. Aid from family (count only aid that is certain)   _____
11. Social Security
      11a. Lump-sum death benefit   _____
      11b. Benefit for each survivor   _____
      11c. Maximum family benefit   _____
      11d. Benefit for 3 or more survivors
           (enter amount on line 11c)   _____
      11e. Number of years you will have
           3 or more survivors   _____
      11f. Multiply line 11d by line 11e   _____
      11g. Benefit for 2 survivors (multi-
           ply line 11b by 2)   _____
      11h. Number of years you will have
           2 survivors   _____
      11i. Multiply line 11g by line 11h   _____
      11j. Benefits for 1 survivor (enter
           amount on line 11b)   _____
      11k. Number of years you will have
           1 survivor   _____
      11l. Multiply line 11j by line 11k   _____
      11m. Total Social Security (add lines
           11a, 11f, 11g, and 11l)   _____
12. Total family resources available   _____
13. Less contributions to others in will (i.e., specific gifts of
    money or property to nonfamily members or to charity)   _____
14. Net total family resources available after death   _____
Life insurance needed (subtract line 14, part II, from line 14a,
part I) $_____

Appendix L

Monthly Savings Needed to Reach Desired Amounts at Retirement

At 6% compounded annually

Age now	Years to retirement	Months to retirement	Desired amount		
			$50,000	$100,000	$200,000
40	25	300	74	147	294
45	20	240	110	219	439
50	15	180	173	347	694
55	10	120	306	612	1,225
60	5	60	716	1,432	2,864

At 10% compounded annually

Age now	Years to retirement	Months to retirement	Desired amount		
			$50,000	$100,000	$200,000
40	25	300	40	80	161
45	20	240	69	138	276
50	15	180	124	249	498
55	10	120	248	496	992
60	5	60	647	1,295	2,590

At 12% compounded annually

Age now	Years to retirement	Months to retirement	Desired amount		
			$50,000	$100,000	$200,000
40	25	300	29	59	117
45	20	240	54	109	217
50	15	180	105	210	420
55	10	120	223	446	892
60	5	60	616	1,232	2,463

Example: To have $200,000 at retirement, a forty-year-old person must save $117 per month if the savings will earn 12% interest.

Glossary

Adjusted gross estate—amount upon which federal estate tax is levied after deductions are taken from the gross estate.

Administrator—the individual or institution appointed by the court to administer the estate of a person who died without a will or whose will did not designate an executor or whose designated executor could not or would not serve.

Agent—one who acts for another.

Annual exclusion—the $10,000 which the Internal Revenue Code permits to be given to each donee free of the federal gift tax each year. (The amount is $20,000 if the donor's spouse joins in the gift.)

Annual exemption amount—amount of earnings allowed Social Security recipient in one year without reducing Social Security benefits.

Annuity—the periodic payment of a specific sum of money for life or for a designated period of time.

At-risk rule—the rule that prohibits an investor from taking a deduction for any amount that exceeds the amount of his investment.

Attorney-in-fact—a legal agent appointed to act for another in a power of attorney.

Beneficiary—one for whose benefit a trust is established or to whom a bequest is made in a will.

Bequest—a gift made in a will.

Board-certified physician—a medical doctor who has taken additional training in his field and has passed an examination given by that specialty's board of examiners.

Bond—an evidence of debt of a corporation or governmental body.

Capacity—soundness of mind required to execute a will.

Capital assets—all property except business inventory, business property, accounts or notes receivable, artistic creations of the taxpayer, and certain US government obligations.

Capital gain—gain from the sale of a capital asset.

Cash value—the cash-reserve element of permanent life insurance which is created with the excess premium charged above the cost of "pure" protection or term insurance.

Charitable deduction—a deduction from gross income or gross estate for contribution to charity.

Clifford trust—a type of trust, recognized by the IRS, to which income-producing property may be conveyed for a period of at least ten years, during which time the income from the trust is taxed to the beneficiary of the trust. Also known as a short-term trust, ten-year trust, or reversionary trust.

Codicil—a formal amendment to a will.

Collectibles—assets collected for their esthetic value as well as their monetary worth.

Commodity trading—trading in future agreements to buy or sell cattle, copper, pork bellies, Treasury bills, and the like at a specified date.

Condominium—a form of ownership of real property in which you own individual living units and share ownership of the hallways, grounds, and other common areas with other owners of individual units.

Credits—a dollar-for-dollar subtraction from tax liability. A $100 credit saves $100 in taxes, regardless of tax bracket.

Decedent—a deceased person.

Deduction—amounts allowed to be subtracted from gross income or gross estate in order to arrive at taxable income or taxable estate.

Deferral—a means of sheltering income from taxation by deferring the reporting of income during high-tax years until a period of lower taxation (such as retirement).

Defined-benefit plan—a pension plan in which the amount of your retirement benefits is determined in advance but the amount of your contributions to the plan varies, depending on projections of how many employees are to receive benefits and how much the benefits will be.

Defined-contribution plan—a pension plan in which the amount of your retirement benefits is not known but the amount of your contributions to the plan is fixed. Also known as a profit-sharing plan.

Depreciation—charges permitted to be deducted against earnings from an asset to reflect the asset's decline in value as it "wears out." Dépreciation is a bookkeeping entry only and does not represent any actual money payment or loss.

Direct-deposit system—a system that allows a Social Security check to be mailed directly to your bank or savings and loan institution for deposit to your account.

Discount—the amount by which a stock or bond may be purchased below its par or face value.

Discretionary trust—a trust under which the trustee has absolute discretion as to how much (if *any*) income or principal shall be paid over to the beneficiary.

Diversify—spread investment funds among a number of investments.

Dividend—a payment by a corporation to be distributed among the shareholders of the corporation. In life insurance terminology, a dividend is a refund of part of the premium paid, reflecting the company's earnings for the year.

Donee—the person who receives a gift; also, a person given authority under a power of appointment.

Donor—the person who makes a gift.

Duplex—a two-family home.

Durable power of attorney—a power of attorney which, by state law and in accordance with the terms of the instrument, is not revoked by the incompetence of the grantor of the power.

Endowment life insurance—a type of life insurance on which a high premium is paid for a limited term. At the end of the term, the cash value of the policy equals the face amount of the policy. The face amount of the policy is paid to the insured when the policy matures if it has not already been paid out to beneficiaries on the insured's death.

ERISA—the Employee Retirement Income Security Act of 1974.

Estate tax—a tax levied against the entire estate of a decedent at death.

Exclusion ratio—the percentage of an annuity that escapes taxation because it represents the portion of the annuity you have purchased with aftertax dollars.

Executor—an individual or institution designated in a will to administer the estate of a person who has died.

Exemption—the deduction allowed from gross income for the taxpayer and persons cared for or supported by the taxpayer.

Family practice—a medical specialty which includes general practitioners who spend three years following medical school learning to provide basic medical care to all family members.

FICA—Federal Insurance Contributions Act. These initials on a worker's paycheck identify the amount paid for Social Security.

General partner—individuals in a partnership who are involved in the management of the partnership and are fully and personally responsible for the partnership's losses or liabilities.

Generation-skipping transfer tax—a tax on the transfer of assets to members of a younger generation which would not otherwise be subject to transfer tax.

Gift tax—a tax on lifetime transfers of assets.

Gross estate—the entire estate of a decedent, before any deductions are made.

Gross income—the entire income of a taxpayer, before any deductions are made.

Holographic will—a will written entirely in the handwriting of the person making the will; not valid in all states.

HR-10 plan—see Keogh retirement plan.

Income averaging—a method of calculating income tax which allows an individual to take a small tax break after a year of unusually high income following four years of substantially lower income.

Inheritance tax—a tax imposed upon the beneficiary of an inheritance, often with the rate increasing as the beneficiary is further from the deceased in relationship.

Integration—the deduction by an employer of an amount equal to up to half of a retiree's monthly Social Security retirement benefit from the employee's pension, reflecting the fact that the employer has already paid for half of the employee's Social Security.

In terrorem clause—a clause in a will which provides that any person who contests the will shall not take any interest under the will.

Inter vivos trust—another name for a living trust.

Intestacy—dying without a valid will.

Intestate—one who dies without a valid will.

Investment tax credit—a credit against income tax liability in the year an investment is made in depreciable business property other than buildings.

Individual retirement account—a private pension plan, the contributions to which are tax deductible when invested and taxable when withdrawn after age 59½. Also known as an IRA.

Irrevocable trust—a trust that cannot be altered or revoked by the person who established it.

IRS—the Internal Revenue Service, the agency of the US government that collects taxes.

Itemized deductions—specific personal expenses permitted to be deducted to reduce gross income.

Keogh retirement plan—a pension plan used by self-employed persons, the contributions to which are tax deductible when they are invested and taxable when withdrawn after retirement. Also known as an HR-10 pension plan.

Leverage—the use of borrowed funds to control an asset many times the size of the individual's own investment.

Life estate—an interest in property that lasts only during the owner's lifetime.

Life insurance—a contract between an individual and an insurance company under which the individual agrees to pay a certain amount of money annually, in return for which the insurance company agrees to pay the individual's beneficiaries a specific sum of money in the event of that person's death during the life of the contract.

Life insurance trust—a trust to which an insured person conveys all the incidents of ownership in a policy of life insurance and which is made the beneficiary of the life insurance policy. On the death of the insured, the proceeds of the policy are not includable in his estate for federal estate tax purposes.

Lifetime exclusion—the amount of assets that may be conveyed during lifetime by an individual without incurring federal gift tax liability. After 1986, this amount will be $600,000.

Limited partners—individuals who invest in a partnership and are responsible only to the limit of their investment.

Limited-payment life insurance—a variation on whole life insurance in which premiums are not payable during the insured's entire life but for a limited period of time. The premiums paid are higher than comparable premiums for whole life insurance.

Living trust—a trust established by an individual during his or her lifetime. Also known as an inter vivos trust.

Load fund—a mutual fund sold by salespeople who charge a sales charge or "load."

Long-term capital gain—gain on the sale of a capital asset that is held for longer than one year.

Marginal tax bracket—the percent at which income tax is computed on the last increment of an individual's income. If the last dollar of your income is taxed in the 22% bracket, you are said to be in the 22% marginal tax bracket.

Marital deduction—a deduction for assets passing from one spouse to another during lifetime or on the death of one spouse.

Medicare—hospital and medical insurance funded under Social Security, which helps protect people 65 and older from the high costs of health care.

Minimum-deposit insurance—the use of loan proceeds from a life insurance policy's cash value to pay for the premiums in whole or in part. Interest must be paid to the insurance company for this "loan," but it is tax-deductible.

Mutual fund—an investment organization that invests its funds in the corporate shares of many different businesses.

No-load fund—a type of mutual fund sold directly from the organization without a sales force and for which there is no sales charge.

Nuncupative will—an oral will, valid only for the disposition of personal property under limited circumstances; not valid in all states.

OASI—Old Age and Survivors' Insurance Trust Fund.

Payroll tax—Social Security tax deducted from an individual's paycheck.

Personalty—personal property.

Pour-over will—a will directing that assets in an estate be added to a trust established by the testator during his lifetime or on the death of one spouse.

Power of appointment—authority conferred by a will or other instrument upon another person, known as the donee, to determine who is to receive property or its income.

Power of attorney—a written instrument by which a person names another as his agent (known as the attorney-in-fact) for purposes set out in the instrument.

Premiums—money paid for a contract of insurance.

Probate—the process of administering a decedent's estate.

Progressive tax—a tax in which the rate increases as the amount subject to taxation increases.

Prospectus—a document which offers investors an opportunity to become investors in a project. The prospectus describes the investment opportunity in detail.

Realty—real estate.

Remainder—the portion of an estate that remains after a previous estate has terminated. For example, if a gift is made to Mary for life and then to John, John has a remainder interest. (Mary has a life estate.)

Reversionary trust—another name for a Clifford trust.

Revocable living trust—a trust established by an individual during his lifetime that is freely alterable and revocable.

Rollover—the changing of a funding medium of an IRA. For example, moving your IRA investment from a stock mutual fund to a bond mutual fund is a rollover.

Short-term capital gain—gain from the sale of a capital asset that has been held for less than one year.

Short-term trust—another name for a Clifford trust.

Social Security—a retirement system of the United States government in which each generation of workers funds the retirement payments for the previous generation.

Special power of appointment—a power of appointment which may not be exercised by the donee of the power in favor of himself, his estate, his creditors, or the creditors of his estate.

Spendthrift trust—a trust in which the assets cannot be sold, given away, or otherwise transferred by the beneficiary before they are conveyed to the beneficiary.

Support trust—a trust under which the trustee is to pay over to the beneficiary only so much income as is necessary for the beneficiary's support.

Tax avoidance—any legal means of reducing tax liability.

Tax-deferred dividends—dividends that are reinvested and not taxable until the stock is sold.

Tax evasion—nonpayment of taxes determined to be due to the government. This is a criminal act.

Tax shelters—any means of shielding or sheltering money or assets from taxation by legal methods.

Ten-year trust—another name for a Clifford trust.

Term insurance—a contract of "pure" life insurance (i.e., life insurance with no investment element). Premiums increase as the insured ages and the risk of death becomes greater.

Testacy—dying with a valid will.

Testamentary trust—a trust established by an individual in his will.

Testator—a person who makes a will. "Testator" formerly meant a male who makes a will and "testatrix" a female who makes a will. The common practice now is to use the term "testator" for both sexes.

Totten trust—a deposit of money in a bank or other savings institution in the name of the depositor, in trust for a beneficiary. The trust is revocable during the depositor's lifetime.

Trust—a form of ownership under which one person holds and manages property for the benefit of one or more other persons.

Vested—fixed or absolute. A right that is vested is not subject to being withdrawn.

Whole life insurance—a combination of life insurance protection and investment. The face amount of the policy and the premium remain fixed even though the insured ages and the risk of death increases. In the early days of a whole life policy, the premium is higher than for a comparable term life policy. The difference in premium is used to build up a cash reserve which helps pay for the additional risk in later years.

Will—the document providing for the disposition of a person's estate on death.

Work credits—Social Security "units" that represent a certain minimum amount of earned income in employment covered by the Social Security Act. In 1982, for example, a worker earned one work credit for every $340 of income in a year, up to a maximum of four work credits a year.

Zero bracket amount—a fixed amount of money by which the gross income is automatically reduced when federal income tax is calculated. Formerly known as the standard deduction, the zero bracket amount is used in lieu of itemized deductions.

Index

www.ingramcontent.com/pod-product-compliance
Lightning Source LLC
Chambersburg PA
CBHW020608270326
41927CB00005B/225